Revelation
New heaven on a new earth

by Philip Bender

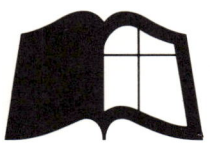

Faith and Life
Bible Studies

Faith and Life Press
Newton, Kansas

Then I saw a new heaven and a new earth . . . And I saw the holy city, new Jerusalem, coming down out of heaven from God . . . and I heard a loud voice from the throne saying, "Behold, the dwelling of God is with human beings. God will dwell with them, and they shall be God's people, and God will indeed be with them (Revelation 21:1-3), *An Inclusive-Language Lectionary, Readings for Year B.*

Copyright © 1985 by Faith and Life Press, Newton, Kansas 67114
Printed in the United States of America
Library of Congress Number 85-81579
International Standard Book Number 0-87303-106-7

The publishers gratefully acknowledge the support and encouragement of the Congregational Resources Board of the Conference of Mennonites in Canada in the development of this book.

This publication may not be reproduced, stored in a retrieval system, or transmitted in whole or in part, in any form by any means, electronic, mechanical, photocopying, recording, or otherwise without prior written permission of Faith and Life Press. Unless otherwise noted, Scripture quotations in this publication are from the Holy Bible, New International Version. Copyright © 1973, 1978, International Bible Society.

Design by John Hiebert
Printing by Mennonite Press, Inc.

New heaven on a new earth
Table of contents

Introduction

SESSION 1. In the Spirit on the Lord's Day (1).........1

SESSION 2. Words for seven churches (2—3)...........9

SESSION 3. Worthy is the Lamb (4—5)...............16

SESSION 4. The great multitude in white robes (6—7)...24

SESSION 5. The seventh seal and the
six trumpets (8—9)......................34

SESSION 6. Sour and sweet for the witnesses (10—11)...43

SESSION 7. Christ defeats the powers of evil (12).......52

SESSION 8. Beasts from sea and earth (13)............58

SESSION 9. Harvest when the earth is ripe (14)........66

SESSION 10. True and just the judgments of God (15—16).73

SESSION 11. Millstone Babylon thrown
into the sea (17—18).....................79

SESSION 12. King of Kings and Lord of Lords (19—20)...89

SESSION 13. God at home in the glistening city (21—22)..99

Introduction

Revelation is a provocative book.

On the one hand, it has aroused confusion, skepticism, and fear. "My spirit cannot accommodate itself to this book," Martin Luther once said. I have had students who have been reluctant to study Revelation because its contents seemed bizarre and threatening.

On the other hand, Revelation often has been the object of curiosity, speculation, and controversy. Throughout the history of the church, many have claimed to see the book's cryptic symbols and scenes being worked out in the events of their time. Our day is no exception.

It is this dramatic yet puzzling symbolism which has made Revelation, for many students of the Bible, discouraging to read and difficult to understand. Several schemes of interpretation have attempted to clarify and expound the book's veiled message. One approach—sometimes called the preterist theory—claims that this message was confined to the first-century church to which John wrote.

On the other extreme, the futurist view holds that the book's contents describe a future epoch of God's work in our world. While this broad approach contains several variations, much popular futurist thinking sees in Revelation a detailed chronology of coming world history. (Sometimes it also is claimed that the church will not be on earth during the events Revelation is believed to forecast.)

Yet a third distinctive line of interpretation does not tie Revelation either to past or future, but sees in it a symbolic description of God's activity in any age.

These varied approaches have led to sharp, sometimes passionate, differences in understanding Revelation's purpose and message. Also, preoccupation by some readers with a few of the book's many symbols and scenes has yielded distorted interpretations, and, more than once, has resulted in unloving disputes between Christians.

Yet Revelation, in spite of its perplexities, remains a book which must be opened, read, and pondered. At its heart it contains nothing more or less than the good news of Jesus Christ for God's people and for the world. Its message is of vital importance for those among us who desire to be faithful disciples of our Lord.

How to use this guide

These lessons have been written with both the individual student and the study group in mind.

In each chapter, the opening paragraphs provide brief introductory material, locating the chapter in the book's larger context. Next, a series of questions about the text, *Getting Started,* lets you gain a basic acquaintance with the chapter's main details. *Commentary* then offers an interpretation of the highlights of the chapter or chapters being studied. Finally, a *Going Deeper* exercise, by means of more study questions, invites you to return to the text for further thought.

You will want to give special attention to the *Going Deeper* resources in discussions where this book is used in group study.

Session 1. In the Spirit on the Lord's Day

Revelation 1

The introduction and opening vision of this chapter lay the foundation for the rest of the Book of Revelation. Here our author will introduce us to the *subject* of Revelation, to the *situation* which called forth its writing, and to the book's *central message*.

At the beginning of our study, we need to make clear the three assumptions which will guide our interpretation of Revelation.

First is the *writing style*. Revelation is written in symbolic language. Animals, objects, natural disasters, even numbers stand for persons, groups, and events. They are symbols, and express or reveal truths which go deeper than their literal, surface meaning. (This writing style was quite well-known in the New Testament period, and is sometimes called apocalyptic, meaning "to reveal.")

John, our author, uses this symbolic writing style lavishly. Many of his symbols are drawn from the Old Testament, and likely would have been familiar to his first readers. Often he casts these symbols in the form of visions. While John may well have seen actual visions, he also writes as a free and creative artist. Under the inspiration of God's Spirit, he has carefully chosen and arranged his many symbols and scenes to express his message.

Second is the *historical circumstance*. Like any book of the Bible, Revelation was written at a specific time and place and for a particular purpose. That background has left its imprint. In a moment, we will examine the situation that John's church faced at the time of his writing. For now, we only note that Revelation cannot be properly understood without a grasp of what was happening behind the scenes in the Roman Empire and John's first-century church.

Third, the *time frame*. The Book of Revelation is much more than a prophecy of the future. In fact, reading it only as a prediction of future history can mislead us and deafen our ears to its message. To be sure, some purely future events are described (mainly in chapters 19—22). But John believed that many of his visions were unfolding in his own day—or that they had *already* happened. What's more, his key visions describe God's activity in the world in *every* generation until Christ reappears.

Revelation, therefore, speaks not only about the future, but also about the present and the past. Our author's main concern is to reveal what happened with the coming of Christ, what God's saving plan for the world involves in the present, and what the climax of that work of redemption will be.

We might sketch the overall time frame of the Book of Revelation in the following way:

Revelation's time

END OF HISTORY
Christ reappears
GOD'S NEW WORLD

1:1   19:10 | 19:11   22:6

GETTING STARTED

Written to take to heart: 1:1-3

1. Think about the word *revelation*. Give an illustration of how we use it in everyday speech. What does the word

seem to mean?

2. To whom is John's revelation directed?

3. To what will John be testifying in this book?

What every eye will see: 1:4-8
1. To whom does John write? _____

2. To whom do the titles in 1:4-5 belong?

3. What event is expected in verse 7? _____

What will be the result? _____

See the voice that was speaking: 1:9-20
1. Where was John when he received his vision?

What clues do you find as to why he was there?

2. What seems to be the central figure of the vision in verses 9-20?

3. What are the main symbols supporting this figure?

_____

_____

4. What number recurs frequently in this chapter?

_____

5. What impression or mood does this vision create for you?

_____

COMMENTARY

The word *revelation* means showing or unveiling truths which may not be immediately apparent. And the truths our author is set to reveal to his readers will concern the *subject* of his book, Jesus Christ.

The Book of Revelation is not a detailed script for future world history. Rather, it is a message about Jesus. It is the revelation of what Jesus Christ *has* done, *is* now doing, and *will* do as God's "faithful witness, the firstborn from the dead, and the ruler of the kings of the earth" (v. 5). Revelation, in a way unique among New Testament writings, proclaims the gospel.

The *situation* of our author and his readers is one of opposition and persecution. John, a church leader who might have been the former disciple of Jesus, writes from the island of Patmos, a Roman prison colony. In his church are brothers and sisters who face the prospect of paying a price for their faith.

John seems to have written around A.D. 95, during the reign of the Roman Emperor Domitian. Ascending to the throne in A.D. 88, Domitian had quickly proclaimed himself "Lord and God."

"I am a divine child of the gods," Domitian had said, "and I demand to be worshiped as such."

Earlier emperors, by also claiming to be divine, had planted the seeds of emperor worship, but under Domitian this practice became widespread. Domitian ordered that statues or portraits of himself be set up in local temples throughout the empire. He also organized a special priesthood to promote and oversee worship of himself.

Each year, unless specifically exempted, Roman subjects were required to report to their temple, burn a pinch of incense before Domitian's replica, and intone, "Caesar is Lord." Failure to do so invited harassment and possible persecution. Refusing to worship the emperor as Lord and God was not just a religious offense against the god which had come to live in the emperor. It was also a political offense, implying disloyalty to the Roman state, and possibly treason.

This requirement to worship the emperor posed a dilemma for serious Christians in the time of Revelation. Could the claims of Christ be accommodated to these pretentious, even blasphemous, claims for Caesar? For these believers, Jesus was their only one true Lord. *"Jesus is Lord"*—that was their basic affirmation of faith. To address the emperor as "Lord and God" seemed to be a betrayal of Jesus. So some Christians, including our author, took a stand: Domitian's demand must be resisted, even at the price of suffering.

An early church tradition tells us that John took leadership in urging Christians to resist bowing down to Domitian. As a result, he was arrested by Roman authorities, tortured, and exiled to the prison colony of Patmos. From his cell, under the inspiration of God's Spirit, he wrote a word to his church as it faced darkening clouds of persecution for its faith. As we read Revelation, we must remember that these historical events are never far in the background.

The *central message* which John delivers to his church is contained in capsule form in the opening vision of 1:12-20. John sees the risen Christ lovingly present with his people. This Christ is a lowly figure. He is not a militant Messiah come to smash his people's enemies, but is rather "one like a son of man" (v. 13), who has died (v. 18).

Yet this lowly Christ is also a mighty Lord! Robed as a king, bearing the features of a judge (vv. 13-14), Christ has seized the keys of death and hell (v. 18), and now holds the destiny of his people in his hands. (v. 20).

So to a church faced with the choice of denying or suffering for its Lord, John in this opening scene announces the heartening good news. "Do not fear the trials which may come upon you. *Jesus*—not Caesar—is Lord. He is here with us. We can hold confidently to our faith, for we are secure in his faithful and trustworthy hands."

GOING DEEPER

1. This chapter offers important teachings about God and Christ. At the beginning of our study, we want to get a good understanding of these teachings, since the rest of Revelation will build on them. One source of teaching is in the *titles* given to God and Christ. In the following exercise, you are to identify the *title, to whom* it is given, and what it seems to *mean* (as best as you can determine from the title itself and from the context).

	TITLE	GIVEN TO	MEANING
1:4c	_____	_____	_____
1:5b	_____	_____	_____
1:5c	_____	_____	_____
1:5d	_____	_____	_____
1:8a	_____	_____	_____

(these are the first and last letters of the Greek alphabet)

1:8c _____ _____ _____

1:17b _____ _____ _____

1:18a _____ _____ _____

2. The second half of verse 5 and verse 6 are important for beginning to understand Revelation's view of the church. Read them carefully and complete the following: Christ's love and blood have _____

_____

making us _____

and _____

in order to _____
Kingdom means a visible earthly society under a king. *Priests* offer worship to God, and also mediate between God and people. With these definitions in mind, state in your own words what ought to be the result of Christ's sacrifice for those who have been freed from sin.

_____

_____

_____

3. The opening vision of Christ in 1:12-20 is most important in Revelation. If you can understand this vision, you will have grasped the central message of the book. Review the vision carefully, using the following key to the symbols. Then state in your own words what this vision reveals about Christ.

Seven = number of wholeness, completeness
   Lampstand = God's people (See Zech. 4:2.)
   Son of man = Christ
   Robe, sash = kingly majesty
   White hair, blazing eyes, double-edged sword = features of judge

Bronze feet, mighty voice = features of divinity
Seven stars = destiny of churches
Key = power, control

4. Recall the situation the first readers of Revelation faced. Are you aware of places in our world today where Christians face a similar situation? How might the teachings of chapter 1 have been good news to John's first readers and to a suffering church today?

Session 2. Words for seven churches

Revelation 2—3

In the bright light of his vision of an exalted Christ who stands with his people (1:12-20), John now turns to address his very earthly churches. These chapters introduce us to a major theme of Revelation—that, in a world which worships false gods and lords, the church is called to a faithful and pure witness to Jesus, who is the world's only true Lord.

GETTING STARTED

Read through chapters 2—3 and complete the chart below.

Praise, warnings, and promises

Church addressed	How is Jesus described?	What is praised?	What is criticized?	What is the warning?	What is the promise?
2:1-7					
2:8-11					

2:12-17

2:18-29

3:1-6

3:7-13

3:14-22

COMMENTARY

These seven churches were not the only ones in this part of the Roman Empire. Colossae, for example, to which Paul had written earlier, lay about ten miles east of Laodicea. Since the number seven symbolizes wholeness or completeness, John probably has selected these particular congregations because they illustrate a good cross-section of the *whole* church.

John writes both as a caring pastor and as a prophet. He reassures his people that Jesus, and not Domitian or any other world ruler, governs their destiny (2:1). Jesus, he assures them, knows his people and their struggle with temptation and trial from within and without (2:2-3, 9-10, 13).

But Jesus also cares deeply about the shortcomings of his people. He sees where his church has accommodated itself to the world and where it has compromised his lordship. Nothing in the churches escapes the blazing eyes (2:18) of Jesus.

Ephesus / cool love: 2:1-7
Ephesus was known as the Light of Asia for its active economic and cultural life. Here the believers have held on to their faith in spite of suffering. They have identified and rejected unworthy leaders. And they repudiated the

lifestyle of the Nicolaitans—probably a Christian sect condoning immorality in the name of freedom from the law.

But the Ephesus church has a flaw. The believers have "forsaken their first love" (2:4). In their zeal for sound leadership, doctrine, and practice, their love for one another has grown cold.

Smyrna / loyal: 2:8-11
In this prosperous seaport city, where several temples honored Rome and the emperor, the church has met hostility from the Jewish population. More suffering can be expected. In spite of these trials, its witness has remained loyal and clear.

Pergamum / inner weakness: 2:12-17
As a Roman provincial capital, site of an important temple to the emperor (probably "Satan's throne" in v. 13), the pressure of emperor worship here likely would have been especially strong. Yet these believers have resisted, with one member being put to death (v. 13).

But Pergamum's strong outward witness to Christ conceals some internal weaknesses. Some members have subscribed to the teaching of the Nicolaitans and of Balaam. The original Balaam had helped lead Israel into sexual immorality and idolatry. (See Num. 25:1-3, 31:16.) Perhaps these disciples of Balaam justified sexual license in the name of Christian freedom. Or, they might have been urging acceptance of the emperor's demands to be worshiped. These new Balaamites might have been saying, "We can honor equally *both* Christ and Caesar as Lord."

Thyatira / Jezebel tempts: 2:18-29
In the church of this commercial center, an infectious spirit of compromise with the world is at work. In spite of commendable Christian works, some believers have succumbed to the influence of "Jezebel."

The original Jezebel, wife of King Ahab, tried to persuade Israel to worship Baal as well as Yahweh. (The story is told in 1 and 2 Kings.) Since "committing adultery" (2:22) is a biblical expression for idolatry and apostasy, this new Jezebel might have been the old temptation to follow another lord—this time not Baal, but Caesar. Jezebel might also have represented the immoral celebrations of the many trade guilds of Thyatira in which Christians may have joined.

Sardis / watchmen sleeping: 3:1-6
Once prosperous, Sardis, at the time John was writing, was a city in decline. Though located on a mountain, it had been captured twice by enemy invaders because its citizens were careless about keeping watchmen posted. In much the same way, the Sardis church is in spiritual decay. Contradicting their outward appearance, most of its members have become so indifferent to the claims of Christ that they are on the brink of spiritual death.

Philadelphia / patient: 3:7-13
This young city was rebuilt after a severe earthquake in A.D. 17. Like Smyrna, its church receives only praise. The Philadelphia believers also have faced hostility from some of their Jewish neighbors, and have met it with a patient, faithful witness to Christ.

Laodicea / lukewarm: 3:14-22
A prosperous center for banking and a wool industry, Laodicea was renowned for its medical school and medicines, notably eye ointment. The city also contained a well-known landmark—a spring of sickening, lukewarm water.

The description of the Laodicean church alludes to these features. In spite of their material wealth, the Christians here are really poor and naked. Even more serious, they are blind to their true state. So completely has this church taken on the character of the world that it has become like its city's tepid, repulsive spring.

To all his churches, Jesus brings a double-edged word of promise and warning: "Repent from your shallow loyalty and worldly involvements. God will yet grant you life. Otherwise, you also will share in the judgment God has reserved for an unbelieving world."

GOING DEEPER

1. Give a descriptive label to each church. In your own words, state its weakness, and what repentance would mean.

	LABEL	WEAKNESS	REPENTANCE
Ephesus	_____	_____	_____
Pergamum	_____	_____	_____
Thyatira	_____	_____	_____
Sardis	_____	_____	_____
Laodicea	_____	_____	_____

2. Why do the congregations at Smyrna and Philadelphia escape rebuke?

_____

_____

3. Recall the specific warnings to the churches if they do not repent. Try to restate these warnings in your own words.

2:5 _____

2:16 _____

2:22 _____

3:3 _____

3:16 _____

4. Recall the promises given to the churches if they do repent and remain faithful to Christ. Restate them in your own words.

2:7 _____

2:11 _____

2:17 _____

2:26-27 _____

3:5 _____

3:12 _____

3:21 _____

5. If a letter such as one of these seven were written to your congregation, for what qualities would Christ commend it?

_____

_____

_____

rebuke it? _____

_____

_____

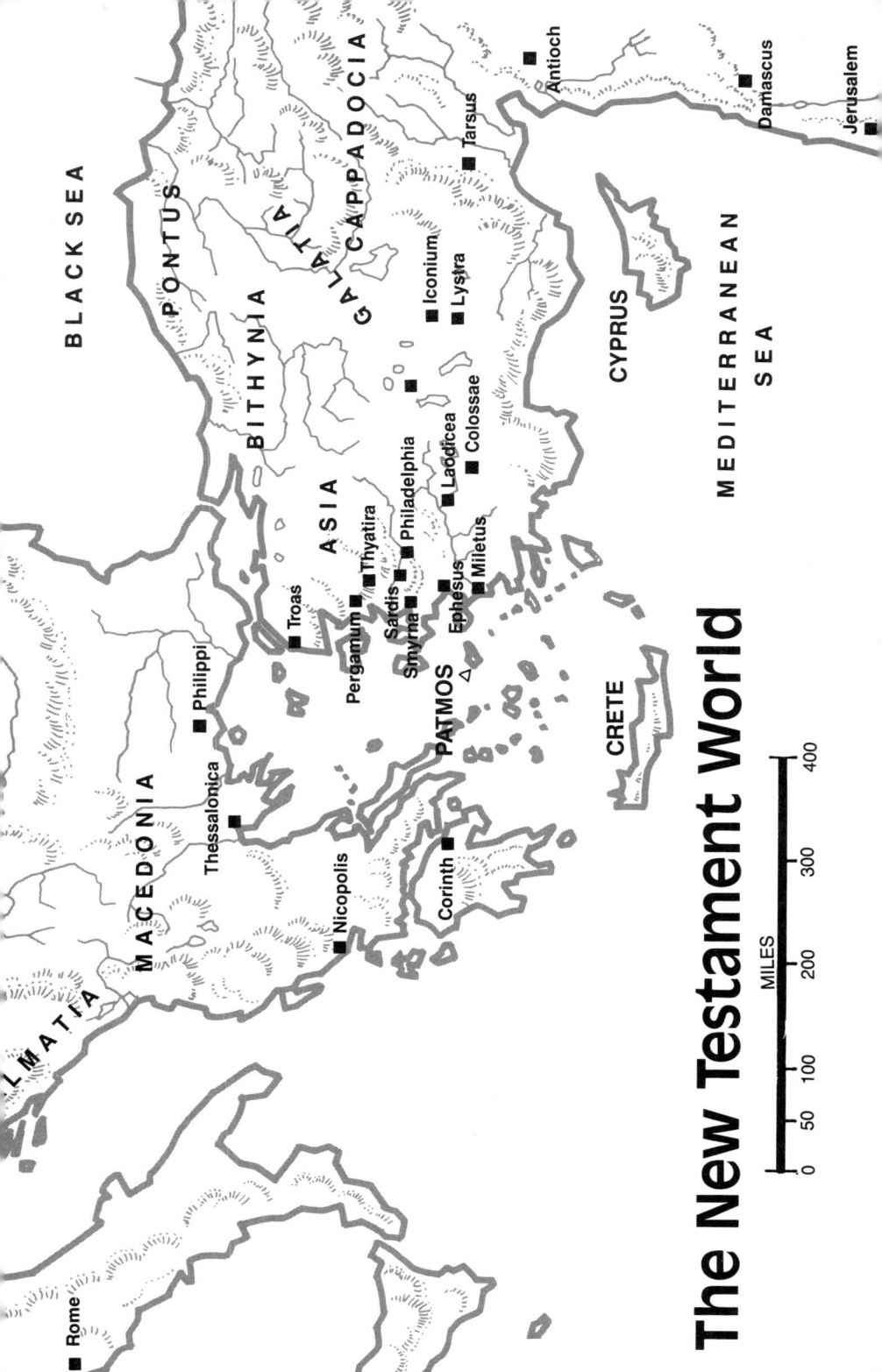

Session 3. Worthy is the Lamb
Revelation 4—5

In contrast to chapters 2—3, where he dealt with the earthly circumstances of his churches, John now writes from the point of view of heaven. From this special point of view, he reveals a profound truth, often not recognized on earth, about who is in control of the universe and of the world's destiny.

These chapters develop the teachings about God and Christ we noticed in chapter 1. They are crucial for grasping the overall message of the Book of Revelation, and for understanding the waves of judgments of the earth which immediately follow (chaps. 6—9).

GETTING STARTED

From the throne in heaven: 4:1-11
1. The heart of this chapter is a great vision of the throne in heaven. On the throne John sees

_____

Encircling the throne is a _____

Surrounding it are _____

on which are seated _____

dressed in _____

Also before the throne are _____

which are the _____

and _____

Standing around the throne are _____

resembling a _____

an _____

a _____

and an _____

2. What do the four living creatures and the twenty-four elders do?

_____

3. List several key words which describe the total impression this vision creates for you.

_____

Songs new and in a loud voice: 5:1-14
1. What new feature enters the vision in 5:1?

_____

2. What is the problem in 5:1-4? _____

_____

3. What enters the vision in 5:6? _____

Describe this figure. _____

_____

4. What does the Lamb do? _____

_____

5. Study the closing choruses of praise using the following chart.

18 / NEW HEAVEN ON A NEW EARTH

	WHO SINGS?	TO WHOM?	KEY WORDS OF PRAISE
5:8-10	_____	_____	_____
5:11-12	_____	_____	_____
5:13	_____	_____	_____

COMMENTARY

God is sovereign: 4:1-11
High above a world in which human rulers blaspheme by calling themselves "Lord and God," the true Lord of hosts reigns.

Two details of John's vision reveal the deeper meaning of God's majestic rule over Creation. First, a *rainbow* encircles the throne. Ever since Noah and the Flood, a rainbow has signified God's gracious covenant with Creation. After the Flood, God had promised never again to destroy the earth. The rainbow was a sign of that promise. (See Gen. 9.)

Now John includes a rainbow in his vision to remind his readers that the God who reigns over the earth loves it and has made a covenant to sustain it. Later in Revelation, when we meet the awful judgments issuing from this throne room, it will be important to remember this rainbow.

Second, before the throne rests what looked like a *sea of glass*, clear as crystal (4:6). It is possible that John intends this sea to stand for evil. In the Old Testament, the sea sometimes is seen as a reservoir of evil. (For some examples, see Ps. 74:13-14, Isa. 27:1.) Later, in Revelation, we will see the evil beasts emerging from the sea (13:1). Also, in God's perfected world, when history reaches its end, the sea will be no more (21:1).

Perhaps, by including the sea in this portrait of the sovereign God, John wishes to express two vital truths about God and evil: 1) God allows evil to exist in a creation which is essentially good, and 2) God remains sovereign over that evil. (Note how the sea seems subdued and motionless before God's throne.)

A heavenly court of twenty-four elders, wearing gold crowns and white garments, surrounds God's heavenly throne. These elders might symbolize all of God's faithful people, both before and after Christ. Also, four living creatures flank the throne. These unusual creatures recall the figures seen in the visions by Ezekiel (Ezek. 1) and Isaiah (Isa. 6), and probably symbolize the whole of creation.

Most important about these elders and creatures is what they do: they worship God. They fill God's chamber with praise. In heaven, if not on earth, John seems to say, the true Lord of the universe is worshiped by the church and by all other creatures.

Christ is Lord: 5:1-14

Next John sees a sealed scroll. To Revelation's first readers, a scroll could have had many meanings: a last will and testament, a prophetic message (for example, Ezek. 2:9), a kingdom's unknown future. Since this scroll is found in God's right hand, we might best understand it as symbolizing God's plan for the world.

But there is a problem. "Who is worthy to break the seals and open the scroll?" (5:2). God requires a helper to implement that plan, but none can be found. Finally, one worthy enough is found. But it is not someone of exceptional greatness and power. That helper is not a Lion, but a Lamb!

Though this Lamb seems powerless and pitiful, appearing to have been slain (5:6), it is alive and strong. It strides forward and seizes the scroll from God's hand. This unseemly Lamb, even though marked with death, has taken charge of the world's destiny. This Lamb can only be Jesus Christ.

Here we see John restating symbolically the heart of the gospel: *Jesus is Lord!* Through his servant-life, death, and resurrection, he has become Lord of the world. Jesus—not Caesar, nor any other human or spiritual power—holds the world's future in his hands.

As the Lamb grasps the scroll from God and prepares to break its seals, all heaven erupts in a chorus of praise. And with the closing scene of "every creature in heaven and on earth and under the earth and on the sea" (v. 13) exalting Jesus as Lord, John foreshadows the world which will be when the scroll is fully opened and God's purposes are complete.

GOING DEEPER

1. The visions of chapters 4—5 draw back the shades of the surface reality of our world to reveal who really controls the universe and guides its destiny. Project yourself back in time to the situation of Revelation's first readers. Looking at the world around you through their eyes, complete the left-hand column. Next, in view of the revelations of these chapters, complete the right-hand column.

Who controls?

	FROM THE POINT OF VIEW OF EARTH	FROM THE POINT OF VIEW OF HEAVEN
Who controls events on earth?	_____	_____
Who sits on great thrones?	_____	_____
Who is clothed in power and glory?	_____	_____
Who is praised as "Lord and God" (v. 11)?	_____	_____

Is a lamb strong or
weak?   _____ _____

Are the suffering
saints defeated or
victorious?   _____ _____

Who is worthy to
receive power,
wealth, wisdom,
strength, honor,
glory, praise?   _____ _____

Before whom do we
fall in worship?   _____ _____

If you had been one of Revelation's first readers, what might these insights you have just made have meant to you?

_____

_____

Lamb for a lion's work
2. What do you associate with a lamb? _____

_____

with a lion? _____

Why do you think John portrays Christ as a lamb rather than a lion? (Consider the larger New Testament view of Christ as you decide on your answer.)

_____

_____

_____

22 / NEW HEAVEN ON A NEW EARTH

3. What do the seven horns and seven eyes add to the picture of the Lamb (5:6b)?

4. What do these chapters suggest about the relationship between God and Christ?

5. In the hymn of praise to the Lamb in 5:9-10, why is the Lamb worthy to implement God's plan for the world?

What else has the blood of the Lamb accomplished?

What insights does verse 10 give into the task of God's people for today?

What promise does verse 10 offer?

6. Summarize in two or three sentences the view of Christ given in chapter 5.

Very nature of a servant
7. Philippians 2:5-11 is one of several larger New Testament descriptions of the person and work of Christ. Read this passage and note the major points about Christ. Try

to find similar points in the picture of Christ in Revelation 5.

PHILIPPIANS 2:5-11   REVELATION 5:1-14

Session 4. The great multitude in white robes

Revelation 6—7

With chapter 6, the contents of the Lamb's scroll begin to be released.

A word here about our author's overall outline might help us chart our way. Although he speaks of seeing visions, John actually has arranged his material in a careful, artistic manner. Earlier, we noted that the time frame of Revelation covers the whole period between the cross and God's new world at the end of history. John's pattern for the next thirteen chapters will describe *four* times, by means of seven *seals* (6:1—8:5), seven *trumpets* (8:6—9:21), seven *scenes* (12:1—14:20), and seven *bowls* (15:1—19:10) how God is at work during this whole time span for the world's redemption.

We should view the scenes which follow in Revelation not as a strict outline of specific events that follow one after the other, but rather as sketches, snapshots, or cartoons which move both forward and backward along the time line, showing *different* parts of the *same* process of salvation and judgment set in motion by Christ.

Often the same scene will be repeated, using different symbols or given in more depth and detail. (The style is not unlike a quick-paced slide show of a summer holiday!) Here and there are glimpses of the future, but only near the end of the book will John's point of view become clearly future.

It is important to be aware of this *repetition* in Revelation. Otherwise, we can misunderstand John's message—or simply get lost!

Just before the seventh item of each series, John has inserted a special word to the church about its place in God's saving purposes. We will see the first of these special words in chapter 7.

We might diagram the pattern of Revelation in the following way:

Seals, trumpets, scenes, and bowls

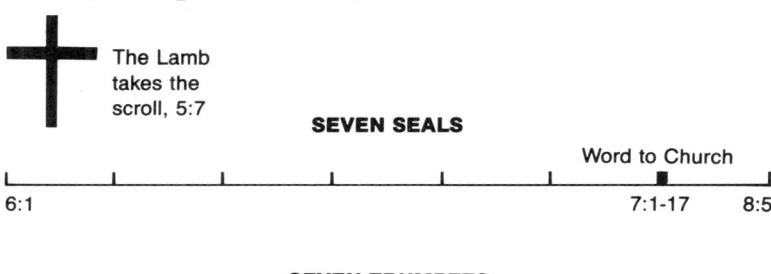

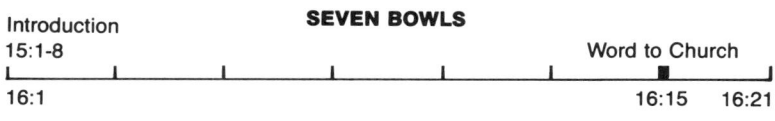

GETTING STARTED

Read carefully through this chapter and complete the following chart.

Scroll unsealed by the Lamb: 6:1-17

SEAL NUMBER   CONTENTS   ACTION OR RESULT

6:1-2 _____ _____ _____

6:3-4 _____ _____ _____

6:5-6 _____ _____ _____

6:7-8 _____ _____ _____

6:9-11 _____ _____ _____

6:12-17 _____ _____ _____

Multitude in white robes: 7:1-17

1. What is the importance of the angel from the east (7:2-4)?

_____

2. What is the total number of those sealed? _____

3. Where do these servants come from? _____

4. What is the makeup of the throng that John sees (7:9)?

5. What seems to be the key word in the chorus of praise (7:10)?

_____

6. Through what has this throng come (7:14-15)?

7. What specific promises are given in 7:16-17?

COMMENTARY

Understanding Revelation's judgments

The judgment scenes for which Revelation is often noted may seem fearsome, grotesque, and endless. They also may seem to describe a period of history which is not ours. To properly grasp their message, we should first note the larger New Testament view of when and how God judges human sin.

Romans 1 is a good place to begin. Here Paul, in a much different style than John's, also speaks about God's judgment. He says that the wrath of God is "revealed from heaven against all godlessness and wickedness of men who suppress the truth by their wickedness" (1:18). God judges sin *now*, Paul says, and not only at the end of time.

And the means by which this judgment is carried out is by God "giving them over" to their sin (1:24, 26, 28). That is, God works against sin now by letting the world reap the bitter fruits of its sinfulness.

The author of Revelation shares Paul's basic view of God's judgment of evil and sin. John will be teaching us that God's plan for the world, begun in Christ, involves bringing down all the defeated powers of sin and evil which continue to resist. This judgment occurs now, in the present, and foreshadows the last judgment at the end of history. Most of Revelation's vivid judgment scenes use symbols to describe the trials a rebellious world brings on itself now and to which God "gives it over."

Two other parts of Revelation's judgment scenes must

be kept in mind. First, their *scope.* John will show that the present judgments of God involve not only individual persons. These judgments aim especially at those rulers, nations, governments, and societies which are built on idolatry and oppress the church. More deeply yet, God's judgment is directed against the dark, underlying powers of evil.

Second, their *purpose.* God's present judgments are for *redemption,* not revenge. They seek to save the world, not destroy it. We must never forget that the seals, trumpets, and bowls of Revelation have their source in a holy throne enfolded by a gracious rainbow, called forth by a nonviolent Lamb slain for the salvation of the world.

The judgment of the seals: 6:1-17

Perhaps we can recognize these mounted riders. The *white* horse and rider represent old humanity's Satan-inspired spirit of arrogance and rebellion, especially as seen in the militarism and conquest of nations. They are followed by a *red* horse, representing war; a *black* horse, symbolizing famine; and a *pale* horse, standing for death.

The cry of the saints: 6:9-11

Under the altar, John sees sisters and brothers who have given their lives for Christ. These faithful martyrs cry out to God, "How long?"—how long until the powers of evil which have killed them are fully conquered? In response, God not only rewards these saints and counsels patience. God also suggests that others too may be called on to give their lives in faithful witness to Christ.

Here we glimpse Revelation's sobering teaching about the role of the church during this present period of God's judgment: the church is called to follow its Lord in bearing the cross. In so doing, it will serve God's plan to save the world.

Nature in upheaval: 6:12-17

This scene echoes several Old Testament prophets' description of God's final judgment of the evil nations at the end of history. (For example, see Joel 2:10, 30-32; Isa. 13:9-22, 34:4; Ezek. 32:7-8; Amos 8:9.) Earthquakes, falling stars, disfiguring of the sun and moon, and other natural catastrophes are symbolic biblical pictures of God's warfare in history against the "rulers . . . authorities . . . powers of this dark world . . . spiritual forces of evil in the heavenly realms" (Eph. 6:12) which work unrighteousness and blemish God's good creation.

Word to the church: 7:1-17
The judgments of the seven seals prompted an urgent question: "who can stand" the wrath of God (6:17)? By using symbols, John intends to answer: those who remain faithful to the Lamb now.

Three interrelated symbols convey this reassurance to the church.

1. *Sealing.* Four angels restrain the winds of God's judgment, so that a fifth can "put a seal on the foreheads of the servants of God" (7:3). Sealing denotes *identity and protection.* The sealing of these servants recalls similar actions in Ezekiel (9:1-11) and Exodus (12:12-13, 21-23), where the faithful of Israel were identified and protected against God's judgment of evil.

Here we must understand the sealing in a spiritual sense. Though they may be caught up in the shock of judgment which God now visits against a rebellious world (seals 1-6), those bearing the seal of God are spiritually secure.

2. *Israel.* The sealed servants are identified as coming from the tribes of Israel (7:4). By Israel, John means the new Israel, or the *church.* Many New Testament writers describe those who have come to faith in Christ—both Jews and Gentiles—using words that apply to the old Israel. The church can be assured of its spiritual security now and in the future as God completes the conquest of evil begun in Christ.

3. *144,000.* How many of the church will *stand?* John's answer: *all* of the Lamb's people, or "144,000" (7:4)! John's symbolic calculation runs as follows: 12 (Old Testament people of God) x 12 (New Testament people of God) x 1,000 ("vastness, without limit") = 144,000. (For 1,000 as a symbol of a vast quantity or as a time which cannot be measured, see Ps. 50:10, 2 Pet. 3:8.)

In summary, the scene of 7:1-8 really restates the gospel: whoever believes in Jesus will be saved!

The closing scene (7:9-17) views this same 144,000 from the point of view of the future. This numberless, universal throng of saints now has passed through the great tribulation (7:14)—that period of history since the cross, when the defeated evil powers war in a final assault against the Lamb and his people. (This tribulation drama will be fully developed in chapters 12—13.)

Erupting in a chorus of praise to God and to the Lamb for their salvation, this future church stands ready to inherit the fully-redeemed world which God has promised and to which they have witnessed.

John has inserted these two scenes of the church just before the seventh—and last—seal in order to reassure and encourage his sisters and brothers in Christ. Though evil may buffet them now, their loyalty to the Lamb in the end will assure them salvation and blessing.

GOING DEEPER

1. Though the six seals bring forth mainly dark disasters, there are two important rays of light we must not overlook. Who is in control of the seals?

What evidence can you find in the first four seals that these judgments are being restrained?

2. In Revelation, white is normally the color of purity, truthfulness, and victory. (Christ will appear on a white horse in 19:11.) Here the lead *evil* horse is white. Why do you think our author has colored it this way?

3. Where do you see these horses and riders in our world today?

4. The fifth seal develops further Revelation's view of the church in the time between the cross and Christ's reappearance. What do you think was the nature of the testimony that those under the altar gave which resulted in their deaths? (Keep in mind Revelation's historical setting.)

Restate in your own words God's reply to their cry for justice (6:10b).

How does this scene help to understand what it means for the church to be the "kingdom and priests" (1:6, 5:10) to which it is called?

5. In the natural disasters of the sixth seal, who is singled out for judgment?

_____

_____

Why do you think they received the most severe judgments of all?

_____

_____

6. An important issue in the interpretation of Revelation is the meaning of Israel. It might help us to see Israel as the church by noting how other New Testament writers also employ Jewish terms to speak of the church. (Being from Jewish heritage, it is understandable that they would express their faith in Christ with familiar words.) Look up the following references and note how the writer describes the church.

Galatians 6:16 _____

James 1:1 _____

1 Peter 2:9 _____

Romans 4:16 _____

Galatians 3:7-9 _____

1 Corinthians 3:16 _____

7. In 7:14, we learn what has enabled the Lamb's people to pass safely through the great tribulation. Who has done the washing of the robes?

_____

In what have these robes been washed?

_____

What color has resulted?

_____

Where have we seen robes of this color before?

What does the color mean?

What is Revelation teaching us about what it means, practically speaking, to wash one's robe "in the blood of the Lamb?"

8. In no more than three sentences, summarize what you understand to be the main message given to the church in chapters 6—7.

Session 5. The seventh seal and the six trumpets

Revelation 8—9

Our last lesson brought us to the seventh—and final—seal of the Lamb's scroll. So we might expect that, with its opening, God's plan for the world will be realized and the Book of Revelation will end.

Such is not the case. The action not only continues, but moves forward under a new symbol: seven *trumpets*.

Here we see, as noted earlier, repetition at work in Revelation. Chapters 8—9 cover much the same ground as 6—7: the period between the cross and God's new world at the end of history. But these chapters also add a deeper dimension to God's present work in history. They respond to the prayer of the saints (seal 5) for the triumph of good over evil.

From this point on, God's judgment of the arrogant and rebellious earthly and spiritual powers, symbolized by the white horse (6:2), will be more clearly in view.

Our author's writing style has become like an orchestra which repeats but develops a simple melody the longer it plays.

This diagram may help us locate where our study has brought us:

From the cross to God's new world

The Lamb takes the scroll, 5:7

SEVEN SEALS

Word to Church

6:1 — 7:1-17 — 8:5

SEVEN TRUMPETS

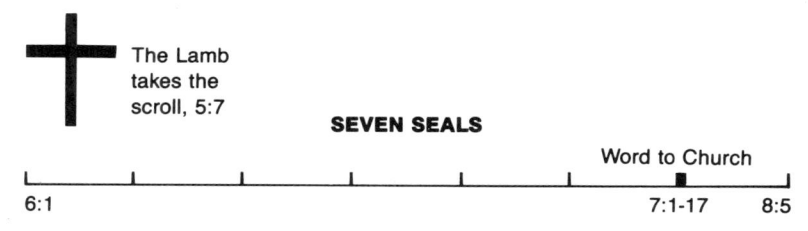

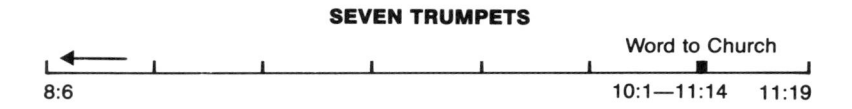

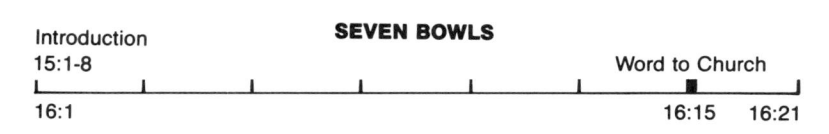

Word to Church

8:6 — 10:1—11:14 — 11:19

SEVEN SCENES

Word to Church

12:1 — 14:13 — 14:20

Introduction 15:1-8

SEVEN BOWLS

Word to Church

16:1 — 16:15 — 16:21

BOWLS EXPANSION

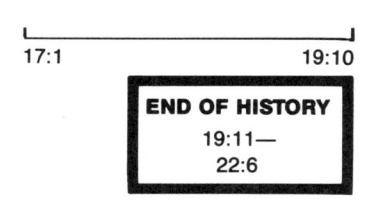

17:1 — 19:10

> **END OF HISTORY**
> 19:11— 22:6

GETTING STARTED

1. What happens with the opening of the seventh seal (8:1)?

2. What does the angel at the altar mix with the incense (8:3-5)?

3. Complete the first *three* columns of the following chart. (We'll do the fourth one later.)

Trumpets and plagues

TRUMPET NUMBER	CONTENTS	RESULT OF JUDGMENT	EXODUS PLAGUES
8:7			Exod. 9:23 / #7
8:8-9			Exod. 7:20 / #1
8:10-11			
8:12			Exod. 10:21 / #9
9:1			Exod. 10:1-20 / #8
9:13			Exod. 12:29-30 / #10

4. Look more closely at the locusts (9:1-11).

Where do they come from? _____

What are their faces like? _____

Who is their king? _____

Whom do they attack? _____

How do their victims regard them? _____

_____

COMMENTARY

The seventh seal: 8:1-2
In sharp contrast to the tumult of the first six seals, suddenly there is silence. Probably this silence is intended to accent the prayer scene which follows.

The power of prayer: 8:3-5
Here John impresses upon his church the potential power of its worship. Before the heavenly altar, an angel adds incense to the prayers of the saints, and the mixture rises to God. Next, the angel fills a censer with fire and flings it to earth. At that moment, thunder, lightning, and earthquake—symbols of God's presence and judgment—erupt.

This scene builds on seal 5, where the martyred saints pray that God might soon act to destroy the persecuting evil powers (6:10). Our author here reassures the church that its prayer for the final defeat of evil is not fruitless. The prayers of the Lamb's people—as he will show in the trumpet series—also contribute directly to the working out of God's redemptive purpose in the world.

Six trumpets: judgment before exodus: 8:6—9:19
This new series of judgments against the earth in response to the church's prayer brings to mind the story of the Exodus from Egypt. Before God, through Moses, led Israel out of bondage, ten plagues of nature were inflicted on Pharaoh's land and people. (The story is found in Exod. 7—11.) This long series of judgments was made necessary because of Pharaoh's continuing refusal to repent of his hardness of heart and let God's people go free.

John saw his church facing a slavery not unlike that of Israel of old. In his day, a new Pharaoh—Domitian—had turned against God's people, because they had pledged allegiance to Jesus as Lord. (Later generations of the church have had to face their own Pharaohs.)

But John also believed that God, as before in Egypt, now lifted a hand of judgment against this new Pharaoh—and also against that Pharaoh's sinister spiritual master. With generous allusions to the Exodus plagues, his scenes in chapter 8 announce God's judgment of the new Pharaohs who desecrate the earth and oppress the church. These judgments in history, our author believed, were the necessary prelude to the new promised land which would later follow.

Face to face with evil: the locusts: 9:1-11
A closer look at one particular scene—the locust plague—offers deeper insight into how God deals with the powers of evil.

1. *The locusts have a satanic origin.* They rise from the Abyss. In Revelation, the Abyss is the abode of Satan. The evil powers generating these hordes are the "spiritual forces in the heavenly realms" identified as the Christian's primary enemy (Eph. 6:12).

2. *The locusts take human form.* Though animated by the evil powers, these locusts take on flesh. Note carefully the close-up in 9:7. They have human faces. Also observe their king: Abaddon, also known as Apollyon (9:11). Here John makes a deliberate play on words. "Abaddon" and "Apollyon" both mean "destroyer." But Apollyon also alludes to the god Apollo, who Domitian believed himself to be! The meaning is clear: these hosts of evil are led by human lords like Domitian who play God on earth. They represent humanity following these arrogant earthly lords in rebellion against the true Lord of the universe.

3. *The locusts are controlled by God.* Even though they work destruction, the locusts are fully subject to God's rule. They come forth from the Abyss only because a key *was given* (by God!) to the doorkeeper star (9:1-2), and can afflict only because such power also *was given* them (9:3).

4. *The locusts are the instrument of God's judgment of evil.* Note whom they attack: only the enemies of God (9:4). Though they represent human rebellion against God, these locusts, in God's providence, have become the means by which God judges that rebellion. They dramatize vividly Paul's understanding of God's judgment we noted earlier—that God judges sin by *giving us over* to its destruction.

5. *God's purpose in judgment remains repentance and redemption.* The conclusion to the trumpet judgments in 9:20-21 repeats this truth. Also, out of grace, God now restrains those judgments; the locusts are not permitted to kill, but only *torture* their victims, and then only for five months (9:5). God limits the ruin produced by sin so that the world might have maximum time for repentance.

6. *As God's judgment intensifies, so does the resistance of evil.* Note that the most terrible and extravagant symbols of evil come toward the end of the series (trumpets five and six). By increasing the intenseness of each image, scene after scene, John suggests another truth: that the longer sin persists without repentance, the more severe will be God's judgment of it. (The whole Book of Revelation is arranged in the same way, the later judgment scenes becoming ever more intense.)

Yet note also that, at the end of the judgments, *there was no repentance* (9:20-21). John seems to imply that even the most severe judgments of God will not necessarily subdue a defiant world's rebellion. That rebellion by some may only increase. Our author will eventually show us that only a new, direct intervention of God in the course of this world's history will finally quell that resistance.

Thinking with symbols

It bears repeating once more that John expresses these truths about God and evil *in symbols.* He works much like the editorial page cartoonist of a newspaper, who comments on the people and events of the news through lively, often exaggerated, drawings.

John's cartoons of devouring locusts and massive cavalry from the east would have made sense to Revelation's first readers. Joel in the Old Testament earlier had likened God's judgment to a locust plague (Joel 2), while an army from beyond the Euphrates would have been a good symbol of disaster for the citizens of Rome—their feared enemy, the Parthians, actually lived there!

We go astray today when we look only for literal fulfillments of these visions, such as grave natural disasters, plagues of insects, or an invasion from Asia. To be sure, God can—and no doubt does—use natural disasters and invasions to judge our sin and lead us to repentance.

Yet the meaning of Revelation's judgment scenes runs deeper than what appears on the surface. We ought to read these visions and ask: where are the rebellious Pharaohs today who defy God and oppress the Lamb's people? How is God visiting plagues of judgment on the world today because of its rebellion? How might a devouring locust, a falling star, or an infinite cavalry be fitting symbols for the destructive consequences of sin God allows me, my nation, my church, my world to experience today?

And, of course, let us always ask: what would repentance mean?

Our author challenges us to see how his symbolic message is being worked out in our time.

GOING DEEPER

1. Let's look more closely and see how these judgments resemble the Exodus plagues. Go back to the chart on page 36. Complete the fourth column by noting the plagues described in the Exodus references. Compare these findings to your earlier observations about the trumpet judgments.

2. What do you suppose the saints are praying for in 8:3-5? (Recall 6:9-11.)

Is this prayer heard in your church today? Why or why not?

3. List the sins from which humanity did not repent (9:20-21).

Knowing the background of Revelation, what form would some of these sins probably have taken in John's day?

What concrete forms might they take in our day?

4. If you were to draw a symbol for human rebellion against God today, what would it be? (Try *drawing* it in the space below!)

5. Why do you suppose humanity, in spite of the judgments pictured here, still does not repent?

_____

_____

What evidence do you see that our world today remains hard of heart in spite of the signs of judgment God visits upon it?

_____

6. These scenes also remind us that it is only God's grace that restrains the judgment humanity brings on itself. Where can you see evidence of God's grace amidst the evil of the world?

_____

_____

_____

Session 6. Sour and sweet for the witnesses

Revelation 10—11

What about the church during the present period of God's redemptive judgments? What can it expect? What is its calling? To these pertinent questions, our author now turns.

In the seals judgment series (chap. 6), John inserted a special word to the church (chap. 7) just before the seventh and last seal. Now, on the threshold of the seventh trumpet, he pauses to do the same.

The diagram below might help us locate these chapters in Revelation's larger pattern.

History with special words for the church

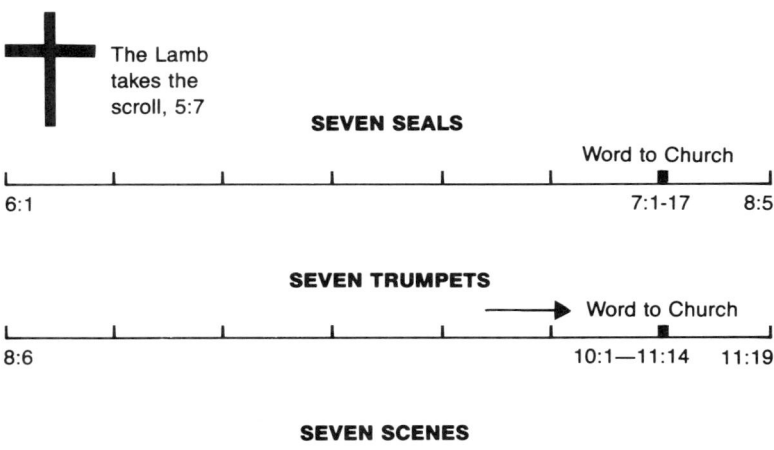

The Lamb takes the scroll, 5:7

SEVEN SEALS

Word to Church

6:1   7:1-17   8:5

SEVEN TRUMPETS

→ Word to Church

8:6   10:1—11:14   11:19

SEVEN SCENES

Word to Church

12:1   14:13   14:20

44 / NEW HEAVEN ON A NEW EARTH

```
Introduction            SEVEN BOWLS
15:1-8                                    Word to Church
└────┴────┴────┴────┴────┴────┴────■────┘
16:1                                   16:15   16:21

                        BOWLS EXPANSION
                        └──────────────┘
                        17:1           19:10

                        ┌──────────────┐
                        │ END OF HISTORY│
                        │   19:11—     │
                        │   22:6       │
                        └──────────────┘
```

GETTING STARTED

The angel and the little scroll: 10:1-11
1. What does John see descending?

_____

What does it hold? _____

Where have we seen one of these before?

_____

2. What command does the voice from heaven give to John?

_____

3. What does the angel order John to do with the scroll?

_____

4. What happens to John after he obeys the command?

_____

5. After this, what new orders does John receive?

_____

The fiery witnesses: 11:1-6
6. John is commanded to measure the _____

He must not measure the _____

It has been given over to the _____
who will trample on the _____
for _____
Power will be given to _____
They will _____
for a time of _____
These who stand before the Lord of the earth are
_____ and _____
If anyone would harm them, those enemies are
_____

These men have power to _____
and to _____

The second woe: 11:7-14
1. What will happen to the two witnesses after their prophesying?
_____

   2. Where will they lie?_____
   3. How will the inhabitants of the earth react to their fate?
_____

   4. What happens to the witnesses after three and a half days?
_____

   5. What happens at the same hour on earth?
_____
_____

Open the temple in heaven: 11:15-19

1. When the seventh trumpet sounds, who, according to the heavenly voices, has become king on earth?

2. Why do the twenty-four elders praise God?

3. According to the praise of the twenty-four elders, what is about to happen to the nations?

to the dead? _____

to God's servants and saints? _____

to the destroyers of the earth? _____

4. What seems to be the central item of the closing scene (11:19)?

COMMENTARY

A new scroll and call: 10:1-11
One feature dominates in this word to the church: a "little scroll" (10:2), which an angel delivers to John. With this scroll comes a new command to prophesy.

Recall that the earlier scroll of chapter 5 symbolized God's redemptive plan for the world, which the Lamb has put to work. Here the new scroll also suggests a plan or destiny. Because it is a *little* scroll, delivered by an angel bearing the features of God (cloud, rainbow, sun, fire, thunderous voice), we can assume that its contents concern something that was in the larger scroll of God's redemptive plan.

John hears voices, but is commanded not to write down

their message. An element of mystery surrounds the working out of God's purposes for the world.

After assuring that God's will for creation will indeed soon be fulfilled, the angel instructs John to eat the scroll. This command recalls a similar order to Ezekiel, when he received his call to speak the word of God to Israel (Ezek. 2:8). John must first fully absorb this new revelation from God before speaking it.

Obeying, John discovers that the angel was right—the scroll is both sour and sweet. The new word from God which John is called to transmit contains both pain and joy, warning and promise.

The church's sour/sweet calling: 11:1-19
John again uses many images from the Old Testament and from his Jewish heritage to reveal the church's present calling.

1. *The church's witness will be protected* (11:1-6). During the time of its mission, the church ("temple") will know the protection ("measuring") of God. Though the church can expect to be threatened and trampled by the powers of evil, God will assure and safeguard its witness.

The nature of this witness will be to speak powerfully and prophetically the word of God to the world. As it fulfills its calling, the faithful church will resemble Elijah and Moses (11:6). These prophets of old spoke the word of God not only verbally, but by means of signs (drought and plague) which spelled God's judgment.

The time of this witness will be "42 months" (11:2), or "1260 days" (11:3). (Each of these equals three and a half years.) These are symbols for the *entire* period between the cross and the reappearance of Christ. They are derived from the time of the reign of Daniel's evil emperor (Dan. 7:25). Because John's circumstances resembled Daniel's, who also faced an anti-God oppressor; and because John foresaw the faithful church facing a similar fate until Christ reappears, three and a half must have seemed a fitting symbol to describe the time of the church's suffering witness to Christ.

Age of the church's witness for Christ

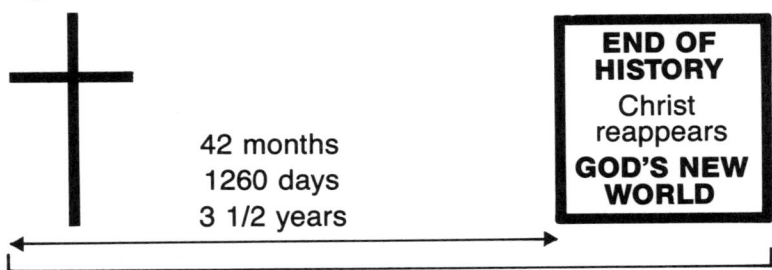

```
                                  ┌─────────────┐
                                  │  END OF     │
     ✝                            │  HISTORY    │
                                  │   Christ    │
              42 months           │  reappears  │
              1260 days           │ GOD'S NEW   │
              3 1/2 years         │   WORLD     │
                                  └─────────────┘
     ←─────────────────────────→
```

2. *The church can expect to suffer* (11:7-10). The *sour* word for the church is that its prophetic witness to the Lamb will provoke the fury of the beast (11:7)—symbol of the earthly powers of evil which now oppose God. From a wicked ("Sodom") and enslaving ("Egypt") world ("the great city") (11:8), the church can expect humiliation, suffering, death—in short, tribulation in this world. Because its powerful, prophetic witness had tormented them, the church's apparent defeat will cause evildoers to rejoice. Like its Lord, the church can expect to bear a cross.

3. *The church can anticipate victory* (11:11-14). But God's revelation is also *sweet*. Suffering and death are not the last words for the faithful church. As was true of Jesus on the third day, resurrection for the faithful church is assured. Its present suffering will be swallowed up in eternal life and victory.

Another sweetness in God's word to the faithful church is its part in the plan of God. As a result of its death and resurrection, many glorify God (11:13). John's word seems to be this: a weak and suffering church which follows in the steps of its Lord will turn out to be a vital tool of God's redemption of the world.

The seventh trumpet: 11:15-19
This scene foreshadows the full achievement of God's salvation at the end of time. Now Christ alone is known as Lord, and justice is done. God's law, symbolized by the old Ark of the Covenant, reigns over the earth.

GOING DEEPER

1. Because of the density and difficulty of the symbolism of these chapters, it might be helpful to review the main items. In a few words, state what our author attempts to say with the following:

a little scroll _____

measuring the temple _____

two witnesses _____

42 months/1260 days _____

the beast _____

the great city (Sodom and Egypt) _____

2. Sum up in three sentences or less the main teaching of these chapters.

_____

_____

_____

_____

3. At this point in our study, it would be well to compare Revelation's view of the church with teachings about and experiences of Christ's people found elsewhere in the New Testament. Look up and summarize the following references:

Mark 8:34-35 _____

Mark 13:9-13 _____

John 15:18-21 _____

John 16:33 _____

Acts 14:19 _____

Hebrews 10:32-34 _____

1 Thessalonians 1:6 _____

1 Peter 4:12-17 _____

How do your overall findings of these verses compare with the teaching about the church in Revelation 11?

_____

_____

4. Think back to the seven churches addressed by John in chapters 2—3. Which of those churches would seem to fit the role of the "two witnesses" of chapter 11?

_____

Why? _____

_____

Which seem to fit it the least? _____

_____

Why? _____

How do chapters 10—11 help explain why Christ, in chapters 2—3, was so concerned for loyalty and purity from his churches?

_____

_____

5. Given their circumstances when John wrote, what might these chapters have meant for Revelation's first readers?

6. What might a prophetic witness for Christ on the part of your church look like today?

Session 7. Christ defeats the powers of evil

Revelation 12

Chapters 12—14 make up the central section of Revelation. They contain the prophecy about the larger world that John was commissioned to give in 10:11. Like the seals and trumpets, this section is built around *seven* items—in this case, seven *scenes,* bound together by the drama they develop.

That drama is the victory of Christ over the powers of evil. Each scene employs symbols drawn from the Old Testament and from ancient mythology to portray one part of that ongoing drama which began with the coming of Christ.

Chapter 12 goes to the heart of Revelation's understanding of the work of Christ. As the first two acts of the book's central drama, it pictures the decisive victory of Christ over evil at the cross. It also warns what the faithful church, as a result of its Lord's victory, can now expect.

The diagram below shows where we have come in our study.

Salvation set in motion by Christ

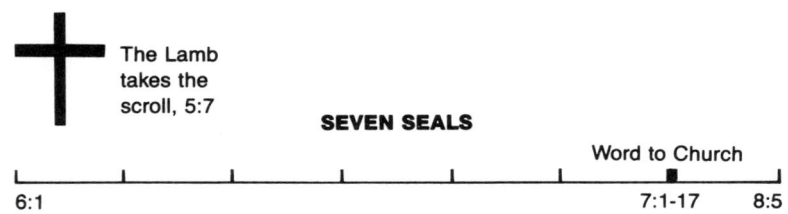

† The Lamb takes the scroll, 5:7

SEVEN SEALS

Word to Church

6:1   7:1-17   8:5

SESSION 7 / 53

SEVEN TRUMPETS

```
|____|____|____|____|____|____■_____|
8:6                          10:1—11:14  11:19
                              Word to Church
```

SEVEN SCENES

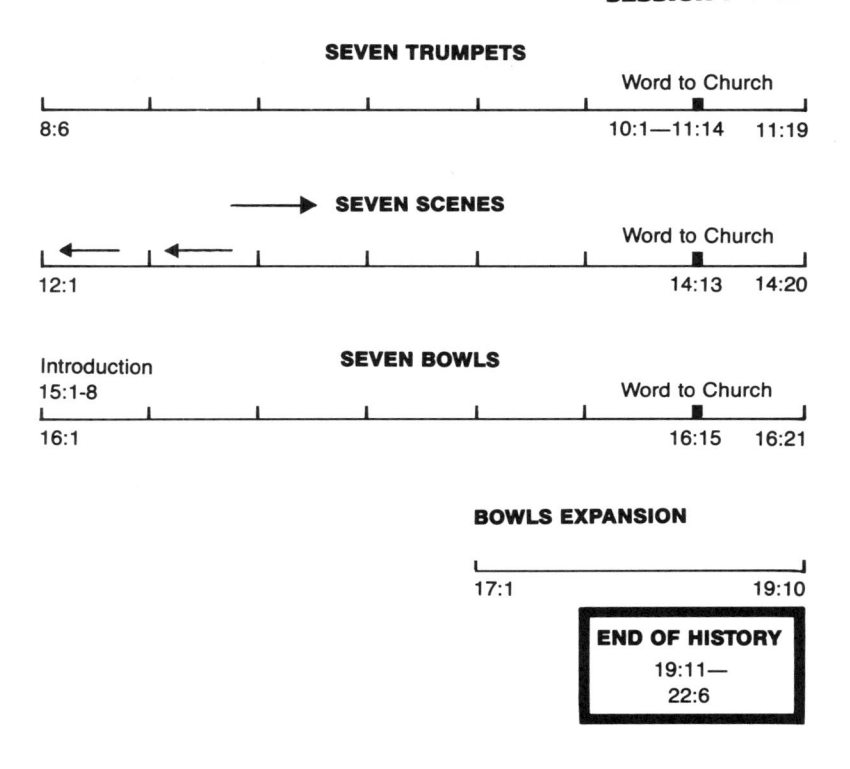

```
|←__|←__|____|____|____|____■____|
12:1                      14:13  14:20
                           Word to Church
```

Introduction   **SEVEN BOWLS**
15:1-8   Word to Church
```
|____|____|____|____|____|____■____|
16:1                      16:15  16:21
```

BOWLS EXPANSION

```
|_____|
17:1                   19:10
```

| END OF HISTORY |
| 19:11— |
| 22:6 |

GETTING STARTED

Read carefully chapter 12. Imagine that you are watching a drama with several scenes. As you watch the first two scenes, keep a running list of the *main characters* and *what they do.*

The victory of Christ/first part

Scene 1: The woman and the dragon: (12:1-6)

VERSE   CHARACTER   ACTION

_____   _____   _____

_____   _____   _____

_____   _____   _____

Scene 2: War in heaven: (12:7-17)

VERSE   CHARACTER   ACTION

COMMENTARY

Represented by the heavenly woman, the people of Israel give birth to their long-awaited Messiah—Jesus Christ—whose mission will involve bringing the nations under his rule (12:1-2, 5a).

From the beginning of his life, Jesus is locked in a bitter struggle with Satan (12:3). But Jesus overcomes the ancient foe, and rises to God's right hand, while God's people receive nurture and protection for the time of tribulation now coming upon them (12:5b-6).

While the conflict between Jesus (now represented by Michael) and Satan climaxed on an earthly cross, their battle was most deeply between spiritual powers in heaven (12:7). This battle was intense; for three days it appeared Satan had won. But then God raised Jesus from the dead, exalted him as Lord, and Satan's domain was overthrown (12:10).

Though mortally wounded by his conqueror, Satan's activity has not ended. Knowing that his doom is sure, he now unleashes a last ferocious offensive against God's people (12:13). While God's spiritual protection surrounds the church during this time of tribulation (12:14), those who faithfully witness to Jesus have become the special victims of Satan's attack.

GOING DEEPER

1. Review the meaning of the main symbols of this chapter:

the woman clothed with the sun _____

the red dragon _____

Michael _____

the war between Michael and the dragon _____

the two wings of a great eagle _____

2. One interpreter has compared the struggle between Satan and Christ at the cross with the World War II battle of D-Day. On D-Day—June 6, 1944—the allied armies stormed the beaches of Normandy. In spite of heavy casualties, they successfully penetrated the Nazi defenses and sent the German army into retreat. However, final victory only came eleven months later, on VE-Day—May 8, 1945.

56 / NEW HEAVEN ON A NEW EARTH

In the interval between these two dates, fighting raged, including defeats for the allies. Yet in larger perspective, those defeats were but temporary setbacks. D-Day had marked the turning point of the war.

Apply this example to the scenes of chapter 12. What event would be like D-Day? _____

_____

What will be V-Day? _____

What is the interval? _____
Where does the church find itself today?

_____

_____

How does the battle strategy of Christ and his people differ from that of the allied armies on D-Day? (See 12:11; also 5:6, 13:9-10.)

_____

_____

3. The rest of the New Testament also interprets the struggle between Satan and Christ as the overthrow of the reign of evil and the enthronement of a new Lord. Look up and summarize the following references:

Luke 10:18-19 _____

John 12:31 _____

Ephesians 1:20-21 _____

Philippians 2:9-11 _____

Colossians 2:15 _____

4. From this chapter, what might Revelation's first readers have learned about why their enemies seemed so powerful?

_____

about why they had to suffer?

How is this same teaching relevant to our time?

Session 8. Beasts from sea and earth

Revelation 13

This chapter continues the drama of Christ's victory over evil. Here the focus is on the most dangerous form which those defeated forces of Satan now take.

This chapter is among the most misunderstood of Revelation. Let us remember that John, first of all, was writing about life in his own day. Only after we grasp the original meaning of these symbols for those days can we apply them to our own time.

GETTING STARTED

The victory of Christ / second part
Continue your observation of Revelation's central drama.

Scene 3: The beast from the sea: (13:1-10)

VERSE	DESCRIPTION	ACTION

Scene 4: The beast from the earth: (13:11-18)

VERSE   DESCRIPTION   ACTION

COMMENTARY

A malicious, multi-headed beast now rises from the sea. Commissioned by the dragon to exercise his power, this beast is distinguished by a healed head wound. Blaspheming God, it wins the worship of many and makes war on the Lamb's people.

Who—or what—is this beast from the sea?
In the first place, for our author, this beast symbolized the Roman Empire. Rome had won the admiration of many citizens through its power, security, and order, inspiring their willing and grateful worship (13:4-8).

Yet at its heart, John believed, the great Roman state embodied Satan. Its emperor Domitian blasphemously called himself "Lord and God" (13:1, 5), and commanded absolute loyalty. Rome also had contempt for the followers of a rival Lord, whose name was Jesus (13:6b-7).

But there is a deeper meaning to this beast. It is older and larger than Rome alone. The wild animals it resembles (13:2) combine features of the four beasts of Daniel 7. For Daniel, much earlier, these monsters had symbolized empires which, like Rome, defied God and persecuted God's people.

We might even discern in this beast a kind of resurrection! Its fatal head wound now healed suggests that it cannot be killed (13:3). In this monster, we meet the church's permanent, insuppressible adversary during the "42 months" between Christ's cross and reappearance (13:5).

In short, this sea beast is a new and deadly expression of the hostility which God and God's people have long known, now appearing in a more concentrated form. It stands for *all* empires and emperors of earth which act like Rome and its arrogant Caesars. The ungodly, beastly state, John is telling us, is Satan's most common form of appearance during Satan's dying but dangerous "end times."

Under the beast's assault, what are the Lamb's people to do? John's answer: they must resist the beast; but they must do so nonviolently, even at the cost of death. By this means, they will overcome the beast (13:10; see also 12:11).

Rome and the beast from the earth

Now a second monster appears. It exercises amazing power, deceiving many to worship the sea beast, who now is identified as 666. It also marks these worshipers, and puts to death those who resist.

This earth beast, first of all, clearly resembles the system which led citizens of the Roman Empire to worship their emperor. At the heart of this system was a network of priests, based in local temples. Through magic and ventriloquism, these priests could work impressive signs, such as making statues of the emperor appear to speak (13:13-15). The priests could dazzle uncritical citizens into worshiping the emperor and could bring harassment and possible death on those who refused (13:15b).

Also preaching the emperor's divine nature in John's day were the Roman coins, which bore the stamp of his image and blasphemous title. It is possible that John had in mind this coinage when he reports that buying and selling were impossible without the hand contacting the mark of the beast of Rome (13:17). Literally, that was the case.

Finally, in the famous 666, we have a numerical code pointing squarely at the emperor. Since the Greek and Hebrew cultures, in those days, had no separate symbols for numbers, the people used letters of their alphabets to express numerical values (such as A=1, B=2, etc.). Written in Hebrew, the letters of the name "Nero Caesar" add up to 666. Nero, an earlier emperor (54-68), was notorious for his persecution of the church, while Caesar was the title of all the emperors. Seeing in the emperor of his own day a reappearance of Nero's spirit, John makes use of this symbol to identify the person whom the earth beast makes the world worship: Domitian, that *new* Nero who sits on the Roman throne and prepares to make war on the church!

Yet there is a deeper level of meaning to this earth beast; it, too, is larger than Rome alone. This beast also can symbolize the tools and tactics of empires and rulers in *any* age which lure citizens into giving them absolute loyalty. Those means used to glorify the state and its heads are plentiful and diverse. Rulers, for example—as some do today—might boastfully use proud titles, such as "Messiah" or "Savior of the People."

Or nations and governments might promote stories, songs, slogans, ceremonies, pledges, rituals, even righteous wars, in which they would identify themselves with God and infer that unconditional devotion is a godly duty. Excessive and uncritical patriotism seems a common device of the modern-day earth beast. And those who dissent can soon be pressured, punished, even killed.

Even though rulers and nations making such grandiose claims are clothed in lies, many people are deceived and offer their absolute obedience—often while claiming belief in a higher God. These citizens form the community of the beast. They are owned by the beast, and take on its identity. That is the meaning of the symbolic mark on their forehead (13:16). The beast's people parallel the people of the Lamb, who also bear the forehead seal of their Lord (7:4).

Finally, 666 too is larger than the Nero-like rulers of Rome. This code symbolizes the beast's idolatrous but deceptive character *wherever* it appears. Recall that 7 is the number of wholeness and perfection—God's number, we could say. Six is *almost* 7—but not quite. It comes close, but forever falls short.

So it is with the state and its rulers who play God on earth. In their effort to be all-powerful, they nearly succeed. Many citizens are taken in by their power, believe their lies, and yield them their worship. But the beastly state forever falls short of its claims. It is *never* the true God; it is always an imposter. In the symbols of Revelation 13, it is always a 6, never a 7.

In brief, scenes 3 and 4 of Revelation's central drama teach us a vital truth: the beasts which oppose the Lamb on earth *do not look like beasts!* Their lamblike horns cover a dragon's voice (13:11). Our author warns us that only those whose eyes and heart are firmly wedded to the Lamb will be able to spot them and resist their deceptions.

GOING DEEPER

1. Review the meaning of the main symbols of this chapter.

	SPECIFIC MEANING IN JOHN'S DAY	GENERAL MEANING IN ANY AGE
the sea beast	_____	_____
the healed head wound	_____	_____
the beast's blasphemies	_____	_____
the earth beast	_____	_____
the mark on the hand and forehead	_____	_____
666	_____	_____

2. An important teaching of Revelation concerns the nature of evil. The following exercise will help you understand more clearly how our author views evil. Note what Revelation and the New Testament tell us about God, Christ, and the Holy Spirit. Then look at the verses that describe the Dragon, Sea Beast, and Earth Beast and note the features mentioned about them.

DRAGON
13:2b _____

_____

_____

GOD
shares power, authority, throne with Christ (12:5, 10)

SEA BEAST
13:1:c _____

13:1d _____

13:3a _____

13:4a _____

13:4b _____

EARTH BEAST

13:12b _____

13:13 _____

13:15a _____

13:16 _____

CHRIST
many crowns (19:12)

bears true name
(19:11, 12, 16)

mark of death
but lives (5:6)

leads humanity
to serve God (1:6)

object of
praise (5:12-13)

HOLY SPIRIT
empowers witness
to Christ
(Acts 1:8)

gives visible
signs (Acts 2:2-4)

means of Jesus'
conception,
ministry
(Luke 1:35, 4:14)

seals believers
for God (Eph.
1:13, 4:30)

3. Recall the basic traits of the Sea Beast and list several of them.

_____

_____

Do you see evidence of this beast anywhere in the world today?

___

4. Recall and list the basic traits of the Earth Beast.

___

What is this beast's relationship to the Sea Beast?

___

Do you see traces of it anywhere today, even in so-called Christian nations?

___

5. How can Christians resist these beasts?

___

___

___

Session 9. Harvest when the earth is ripe
Revelation 14

This chapter concludes the drama of the victory of Christ over evil which began in chapters 12—13.

Consistent with his style, our author has inserted an aside, or special message, to the church just before the seventh scene.

GETTING STARTED

The victory of Christ / third part
Continue your observation of the drama by noting the following:

Scene 5: The Lamb and the 144,000: 14:1-5

VERSE   CHARACTER   ACTION

_____   _____   _____

_____   _____   _____

_____   _____   _____

_____   _____   _____

Scene 6: The three angels: 14:6-13

VERSE   CHARACTER   ACTION

_____   _____   _____

_____   _____   _____

_____   _____   _____

_____   _____   _____

_____   _____   _____

_____   _____   _____

Scene 7: The last harvest: 14:14-20

VERSE   CHARACTER   ACTION

_____   _____   _____

_____   _____   _____

_____   _____   _____

_____   _____   _____

_____   _____   _____

_____   _____   _____

COMMENTARY

The Lamb's redeemed community

After a vision which finds the beast reigning on earth

(13:1-18), John now sees another Lord and another people. On Mount Zion, God's holy hill, the Lamb reigns. Like the beast, the Lamb too has loyal followers—the same 144,000 of chapter 7—who bear its mark and who sing praises before its throne.

These followers have been faithful. They have not repeated the lie of the beast's lordship (14:5). Instead, they have remained undefiled by the world's enticing idolatry (14:4a). In their purity, they stand as a first-fruits offering of humanity to God (14:4c), foreshadowing the larger, redeemed world community which shall offer itself to God when God's saving purposes for the world are complete.

Angel messages of repentance and judgment
Three angels invite the world's repentance and warn of evil's doom. The first (14:6) announces the eternal gospel to "every nation, tribe, language and people"—precisely those who in scene 4 swore their allegiance to the beast (13:7b-8). Even on the threshold of the last judgment, God's grace and forgiveness remain constant and available.

From the second angel (14:8) issues the announcement of Babylon's collapse. Here John introduces a new symbol for the earthly powers of evil. Originally, a powerful empire which took Israel into captivity, Babylon now sums up the character of Rome (and of every other anti-God state since). This haughty, seductive, infectiously evil city, embodying the dying Satan's last earthly resistance to God, now stands on the brink of doom.

A third angel sternly warns the followers of the beast that they court a disaster reminiscent of the judgment of Sodom and Gomorrah (14:9-12). Unless they repent, they will share Babylon's fate.

Promises to the church: 14:13
To the Lamb's loyal people, a voice from heaven interjects two promises. First, their patient and costly witness now will yield eternal blessing and rest. Second, their witness

to Christ will live on and follow them. Perhaps John means that others will come to Christ through their example.

After the harvest—the reign of Christ

A double reaping brings Christ's victory to its climax. The first (14:14-16) is best seen as the harvest that delivers the church into the full life of God's blessed kingdom.

The second, reminding us of the visions in Joel (Joel 3:13) and Isaiah (Isa. 63:3-6), is the harvest of the beast's company which delivers them and their Satanic master into their gruesome judgment.

And so with this scene, the drama begun at the cross is over. Christ's conquest of evil is complete. Justice has come at last to reign on the earth.

GOING DEEPER

1. To get back on board with the drama of these chapters, review the basic teachings of the first four scenes (chaps. 12-13).

Scene 1: _____
_____
_____

Scene 2: _____
_____
_____

Scene 3: _____
_____

_____

_____

Scene 4: _____

_____

_____

_____

2. Now summarize in the same way the themes of these latest scenes.

Scene 5: _____

_____

_____

_____

Scene 6: _____

_____

_____

_____

Aside to the church: _____

_____

_____

Scene 7: _____

_____

_____

3. Compare the name written on the foreheads of the 144,000 with their sealing which we observed earlier in

chapter 7. What does the meaning of this name in this place seem to be?

4. The 144,000 are noted for not having "defiled themselves with women" (14:4). Fornication and adultery are often used in the Bible as figures of speech for idolatry and apostasy. Where in our study have we seen this figure of speech used before?

To what is the sin of Babylon likened (14:8)?

What would the symbol of "defiling themselves with women" have meant to Revelation's first readers?

5. The message of the first angel (14:6-7) suggests that the grace of God is present even as awful judgment approaches. Can you recall where else in Revelation we have seen threads of grace interwoven with dark judgment scenes?

6. For whom has Babylon been a source of corruption?

What does this observation imply about the form sin often takes in our world?

7. For Revelation's first readers, who would have fit the description of those who are warned in 14:9-10?

How will their fate compare with Babylon's? (Glance ahead to 18:18.)

8. To what practical result in one's Christian life should the promise to the church in 14:13 lead?

9. What might the events pictured in scene 7 have meant for Revelation's first readers?

Session 10. True and just the judgments of God

Revelation 15—16

We now encounter the third and final series of Revelation's many judgments—the seven bowls of wrath. Like the seals and trumpets, these bowl judgments illustrate our author's repetition, as they too trace God's activity in history since the time of the cross.

This series, however, accents the growing intensity of both judgment and evil's resistance as God's purposes for the world move ahead.

The key for these chapters was given in the announcement that came with the seventh trumpet (11:15-19). There, voices reported that the time had come for God to reward the saints and destroy the evil powers. The bowl judgments will depict the final triumph of that divine justice.

God at work in world

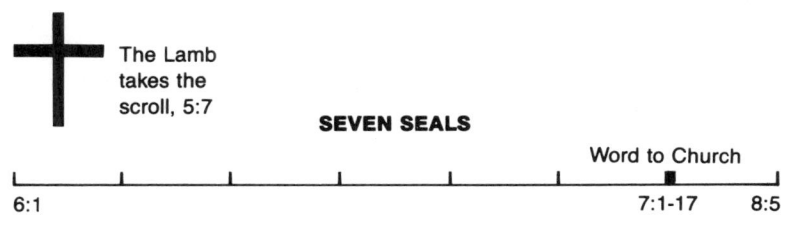

```
✝  The Lamb
   takes the
   scroll, 5:7       SEVEN SEALS
                                      Word to Church
   |____|____|____|____|____|____|____■____|
   6:1                                7:1-17    8:5


                     SEVEN TRUMPETS
                                      Word to Church
   |____|____|____|____|____|____|____■____|
   8:6                                10:1—11:14   11:19
```

74 / NEW HEAVEN ON A NEW EARTH

```
                    SEVEN SCENES
                                    Word to Church
|____|____|____|____|____|____■____|
12:1                          14:13  14:20


Introduction   ──▶ SEVEN BOWLS
15:1-8                              Word to Church
|____|____|____|____|____|____■____|
16:1                          16:15  16:21


                    BOWLS EXPANSION
                    |_____|
                    17:1            19:10

                         ┌─────────────────┐
                         │  END OF HISTORY │
                         │     19:11—      │
                         │      22:6       │
                         └─────────────────┘
```

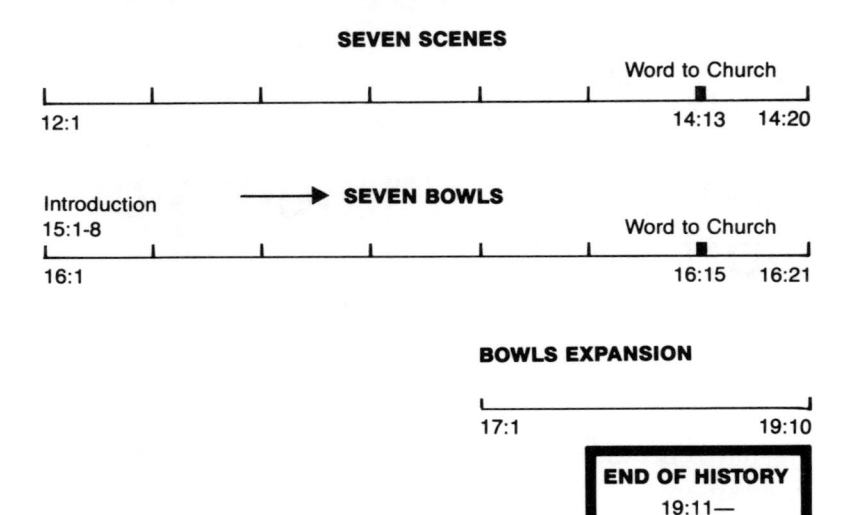

GETTING STARTED

Seven angels with seven plagues: 15:1-8
1. Whom does John see beside the sea?

___

2. What are the main points of their song of praise?

___

3. What are the angels from the temple in heaven about to do?

___

___

Seven bowls of God's wrath: 16:1-21
Read through the bowl judgments and complete the first three columns of this chart. (We'll do the fourth one later.)

BOWL NUMBER	BOWL POURED ON	RESULT	COMPARED TO TRUMPETS: LIKE OR DIFFERENT?
16:2			8:7
16:3			8:8-9
16:4			8:10-11
16:8-9			8:12
16:10-11			9:1-11
16:12-14,16			9:13-20
16:17-21			11:12-19

COMMENTARY

A vision of victory and justice

John foresees the future exodus of his people from their present tribulation under the beast. Like Israel of old, which praised God beside the Red Sea following its redemption from bondage (See Exod. 15.), so the faithful church one day will extol the Lord God Almighty for its final deliverance from the evil one.

Heralding the plagues which will make this deliverance complete, seven angels now emerge from the tabernacle of testimony. This is an allusion to the old wilderness tabernacle, where the tablets of the Law were stored. It suggests that the bowls of wrath about to be outpoured are not God's vengeance, but are the triumph of God's justice and law.

Stiff the resistance of the evil powers
The symbolism of these scenes continues to recall the plagues visited upon a stubborn Pharaoh. Yet some notable developments have taken place.

First, those who are to receive these judgments are clearly singled out as the evil powers and their earthly followers (16:2, 3, 10). They are the hard of heart, those who have disregarded earlier signs of judgment and appeals to repentance.

Second, this human-spiritual coalition of evil resists God to the end. In spite of the agony of their self-destruction, evildoers still do not repent; they even stiffen their resistance to God (16:9, 10b, 11, 21). The deeper Satanic powers do likewise. Note the counterattack against God by the evil trinity and their allies at Armageddon (16:13-14, 16). Armageddon was a famous battlefield in northern Israel. Here our author uses it as a *symbol* of the hardening resistance of Satan and Satan's beastly allies as God's judgment moves towards its end.

Third, the scope of these judgments is no longer limited. Restraint has disappeared, as evil's increased resistance brings intensified judgment. Yet even on the threshold of evil's doom, repentance remains an option (16:9b, 11).

Special word to the church
The word is crisp and succinct: be ready at any moment!

The final judgment of the evil powers will come without special signs and warning. At all times the church must be alert and faithful in its witness to its Lord (16:15).

Crashing end in the seventh bowl
John now glimpses the climax of God's judgment of evil. (This scene will be shown in greater detail in chapters 17—18.) Babylon, the great city symbolizing earthly resistance to the will of God, crashes to defeat, while those who remain unrepentant curse God.

GOING DEEPER

1. Return to the chart you began to complete at the beginning of this lesson (p. 75). Finish the fourth column. Compare the bowl judgments to those seen earlier in the seven trumpets.

2. As a result of this exercise, what conclusions do you draw about the *intensity* of the bowl judgments?

about the ones on whom judgment is poured?

about their response?

3. Read carefully the dialogue between the angel and the altar in 16:5-7. What seems to be the key word in this dialogue?

Where have we heard these voices from the altar before?

Why is it fitting that these voices are reintroduced here?

4. Why do you think this dialogue might be inserted here, after the third bowl, so early in this series?

5. The sixth and seventh items of Revelation's four series usually have shown us a growing intensity both of God's judgment and of evil's resistance. Who or what is the real source of resistance in the sixth scene in this bowls series (16:12-14, 16)?

What are they shown doing?

What does the scene of the seventh bowl (16:17-21) show will be the result of their efforts?

6. What is the key idea in the warning introduced into the scene of the sixth bowl (16:15)?

What does this imply about Christians being able to see the signs and to forecast the time of the Lord's reappearance?

Session 11. Millstone Babylon thrown into the sea

Revelation 17—18

The close of chapter 16 brought us, in John's forward-looking view, to the threshold of the end of history, when God's redemptive purposes for the world will have been completed. From this point on, the action in Revelation will slow considerably, as our author gives us many close-up descriptions of what that end will entail.

These chapters begin that detailed elaboration. They expand the scene of Babylon's destruction given in snapshot form in the seventh bowl of wrath (16:17-21). They also reveal what kinds of people have had a vested interest in this corrupt, worldly city and who now mourn its fall.

More deeply, these chapters offer insights into the nature of evil and of God's judgment in history.

Four times in thirteen chapters

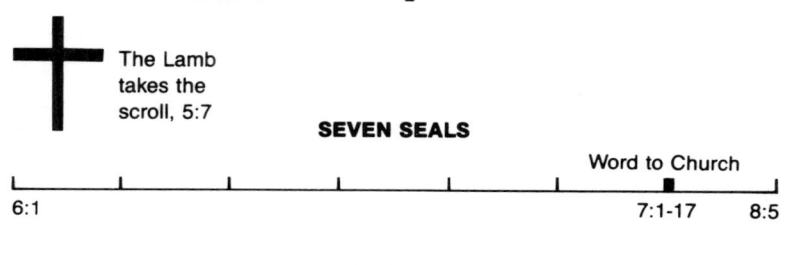

✝ The Lamb takes the scroll, 5:7

SEVEN SEALS

Word to Church

6:1					7:1-17	8:5

SEVEN TRUMPETS

Word to Church

8:6					10:1—11:14	11:19

80 / NEW HEAVEN ON A NEW EARTH

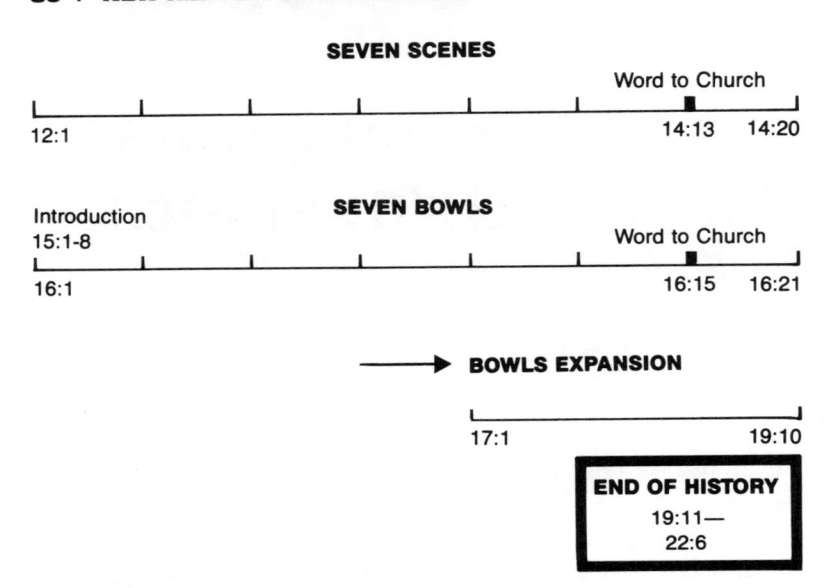

```
                    SEVEN SCENES
                                    Word to Church
|_____|_____|_____|_____|_____|_____■_____|
12:1                                14:13   14:20


Introduction        SEVEN BOWLS
15:1-8                              Word to Church
|_____|_____|_____|_____|_____|_____■_____|
16:1                                16:15   16:21


            ──────▶  BOWLS EXPANSION
                    |_____|
                    17:1                19:10

                            ┌──────────────┐
                            │ END OF HISTORY│
                            │   19:11—     │
                            │    22:6      │
                            └──────────────┘
```

GETTING STARTED

Woman on the scarlet beast: 17:1-6
Note what is said about Babylon the Great:

17:1a: Called the great _____

17:1: Sits on _____

17:3: and on _____

17:4a: Dressed in _____

17:4b: Holds _____

17:5: Is the mother of _____

17:2: Has intoxicated _____

17:6: Is drunk with _____

17:18: Is identified as _____

Mystery woman exposed: 17:7-17
1. List the ways in which the beast is identified.

_____

2. What do the seven hills, seven kings, and eighth king refer to?

3. For how long will the ten horns (kings) have authority?

To whom will they give this authority?

Against whom will they make war?

What will be the outcome?

Why?

4. Who are the waters on whom the prostitute sits?

5. What will the beast and the ten horns (kings) do to the prostitute?

Who allows them to do this?

An angel and voice from heaven: 18:1-8
1. What event does the angel announce?

2. What are the reasons for this judgment?

82 / NEW HEAVEN ON A NEW EARTH

_____

3. What instruction is given to God's people?

_____

Woe for Babylon the Great: 18:9-19

1. Complete the following chart.

WHO MOURNS BABYLON?	REASONS FOR MOURNING
18:9-10	
18:11-17	
18:17b-18	

2. How long does Babylon's fall take?

_____

Death of a great city: 18:20-24

1. What reasons are given here for the judgment of Babylon?

_____

2. How is the death of the city described?

___

___

___

___

COMMENTARY

Babylon up close

In keeping with our author's way of describing evil throughout Revelation, Babylon, the new symbol for Rome, has the character of a wolf in sheep's clothing.

On the surface, Babylon (Rome) was glamorous and appealing. Adorned in outward luxury and glitter (17:4a), she had secured the devotion of the kings and peoples of earth (17:2). Even John seems captivated by her gaudy charm (17:6b).

Inwardly, however, Rome is a demon. She rides atop the beast, and has absorbed its deceitful, blasphemous character. Her strategy is seduction. As the "great prostitute" (17:11), she spreads corruption by enticing kings and earth-dwellers into adultery (idolatry). But against the faithful people of the Lamb, who expose her deceits, she retaliates with bloody vengeance (17:6).

Yet Babylon stands for more than Rome alone. The great harlot city is a symbol of worldliness. It is the outwardly appealing form—political, economic, cultural—of any society whose inner roots are corrupt and whose life has been nurtured by the powers of evil. Though morally bankrupt, the city of worldliness seduces many with its temptations, causing them to turn from the true God and giving it their soul. Because this city is anti-God, the faithful people of the Lamb find in Babylon neither a welcome nor permanent home.

The riddle of the beast: 17:7-14
This puzzling section serves as a parenthesis in the chapter, giving more symbolic clues to the identity of Babylon and the beast.

1. *The beast "once was, now is not, and will come up out of the Abyss and go to his destruction"* (17:8). Recall that God is the one "who is, and who was, and who is to come" (1:4). The beast's title seems to be a deliberate play on and perversion of God's name. Such would fit the beast, who, by nature, imitates God and never fails to amaze many (17:8b). Yet as a counterfeit of the true God, the beast is always headed for destruction.

Also, this title would have fit a popular legend in John's day. That legend was that Emperor Nero, who died by suicide in A.D. 68, would return to life and lead an army from the east in an attack on Rome. Nero, many believed, once *was*, but for a while *was not*, yet perhaps *would come* again. John already has inferred that in Rome and in Emperor Domitian, a new reign of Nero had dawned (13:18). In this title, he could also be warning his readers that a more fully reincarnated Nero was on the horizon.

2. *The beast's seven heads are seven hills and seven kings.* Five kings have fallen, one is, the other—"an eighth king"—is expected, but only for a little while (17:9-11). Seven hills seems a deliberate and literal reference to Rome, which was known as the city on seven hills. Seven kings could symbolize the fullness of Rome's power, seven being the number of completeness. The five fallen kings could be symbols for the truth that Rome's power (or, for us, the power of *all* resistance to God throughout history) is nearly over, due to Christ's victory over Satan at the cross.

The eighth king to come could again reflect John's belief that in Domitian, or possibly in an even more evil successor, the diabolical spirit of the old Nero would be fully restored. Or the riddle of this reference could simply stand for the beast's ability to endure throughout history.

It reappears in new forms as history moves towards its climax. (Recall its healed fatal head wound in 13:3.) Yet every new form of the beast is really the *old* Satanic monster.

3. *Ten kings will join the beast in a futile assault against the Lamb* (17:12-14). This prediction alludes to the sixth bowl of wrath (16:12-14, 16), where we saw the three evil spirits calling the unrepentant earthly powers to a battle at Armageddon. Here John seems to repeat the truth that the powers of evil harden in their resistance to God as God's judgment becomes more severe. But because of the cross, their doom is sure.

The fate of Babylon: 17:15-18
As expected, in the seventh bowl (16:17), Babylon crashes down in judgment. But note *how* it falls—it is ravaged and devoured by the beast who gave it life and by the kings who were its allies (17:16).

Once more our author uses symbols to express his belief that God judges evil now by "giving over" evil to itself. Idolatrous nations and societies sooner or later succumb to fatal decay. Babylon's mortal betrayal by the beast dramatizes the teaching of Paul that "the wages of sin is death" (Rom. 6:23).

Song of doom over Babylon: 18:1-24
This dirge interprets Babylon's fall as the triumph of God's justice on earth. It also exposes those who have had a vested interest in the city.

Babylon has been a wondrous city—wealthy, glamorous, proud, powerful—a thriving center of trade and culture. But Babylon also has been a sinful city. Its gleaming exterior hides a hideously corrupt soul. Its sin has been twofold: it has seduced many into idolatry (18:3), and has persecuted the saints of the Lamb who resisted it (18:24).

Therefore, Babylon has become a city under judgment. For the corruption it has sown, and for its hostility toward the faithful church, it has received its just due.

Some, however, mourn Babylon's fall. The rich and powerful of the earth, who have profited from its evils, have a bitter lament: "Was there ever a city like this great city?" (18:18).

GOING DEEPER

1. In your own words, describe the *outward* character of Babylon.

___

___

2. Babylon is the fourth major symbol for the powers of evil we have seen in Revelation. Recall the other three.

___

How are all four of these symbols similar?

___

___

Use several words to describe Babylon's *inward* nature.

___

What general conclusion can you draw about the nature of evil as Revelation has presented it?

___

___

3. Compare Babylon with *another* woman we have seen—the woman clothed with the sun in chapter 12. Recall what this woman represented.

___

How is the symbol of Babylon like the symbol of the woman clothed with the sun and how is it different?

4. State in your own words why Babylon has been brought down in judgment.

5. How does the fate of Babylon illustrate Revelation's teaching of how God's judgment of evil operates in the world?

6. Observe carefully 17:17. Whose purpose does Babylon fulfill?

Have we seen any earlier indication that the evil powers, in spite of themselves, serve God's purposes?

In a sentence, state what Revelation has taught us about God's providence.

7. What does Babylon's destruction in only "one hour" (18:10, 17, 19) imply about its strength relative to God's?

8. Why, in your own words, do some people mourn Babylon's fall?

9. Where do you see traces of Babylon the Great in our world today?

What would it mean, practically speaking, for God's people to "come out of her" (18:14)?

Session 12. King of Kings and Lord of Lords

Revelation 19—20

With these chapters, Revelation turns more fully toward the future, as John begins to reveal the events which the appearance of Christ will set in motion.

Note that Christ's reappearance itself, in the structure of Revelation, is not the climax of God's redeeming purposes in history (19:11). The description of that grand finale to the work begun in Christ appears in chapter 21. Yet the reappearance of the Lord of the world does form the beginning of this "end."

The symbolic events of these chapters might best be understood as completing the main themes toward which the whole Book of Revelation has been working all along. Now, in these chapters, these acts climax the triumph of God's justice in history toward which the seven bowls (chap. 16) and the collapse of Babylon (chaps. 17—18) have been pointing.

From the cross to God's new world

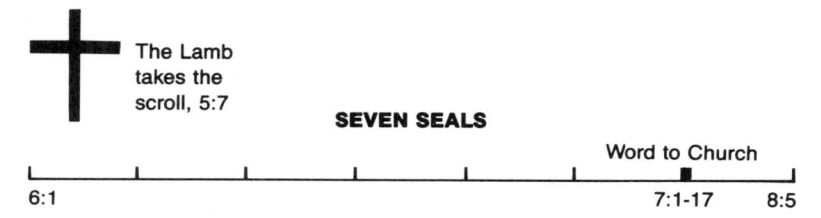

✝ The Lamb takes the scroll, 5:7

SEVEN SEALS

Word to Church

6:1 7:1-17 8:5

SEVEN TRUMPETS

```
|_____|_____|_____|_____|_____|_____Word to Church___|
8:6                                      10:1—11:14  11:19
```

SEVEN SCENES

```
|_____|_____|_____|_____|_____|_____Word to Church___|
12:1                                             14:13  14:20
```

Introduction
15:1-8

SEVEN BOWLS

```
|_____|_____|_____|_____|_____|_____Word to Church___|
16:1                                             16:15  16:21
```

BOWLS EXPANSION

```
|_____|
17:1                    19:10
```

| END OF HISTORY 19:11— 22:6 | 19:11 Christ reappears | GOD'S NEW WORLD 21:1 |

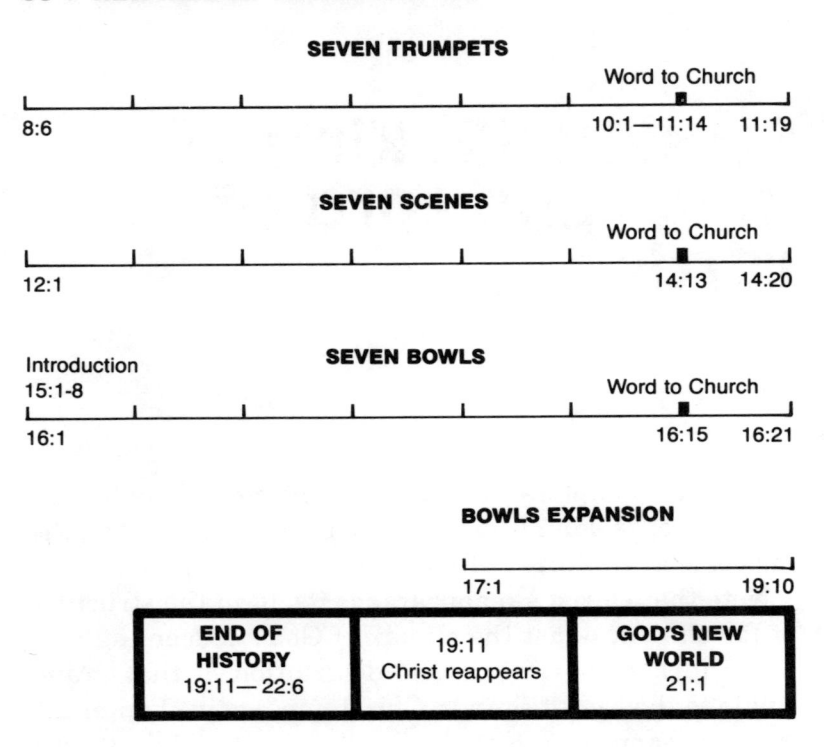

GETTING STARTED

Roar of a great multitude: 19:1-10

1. What shout of praise is heard again and again in this section?

_____

Who is shouting? _____

To whom is their praise directed? _____

2. List the reasons why this multitude is ecstatic with praise.

_____

_____

_____

3. To what event are they looking forward (19:7, 9)?

Six scenes of victory: 19:11—20:15
This section is broken into six quick action-packed scenes. In order to get an overall impression, complete the following chart.

WHAT JOHN SEES	WHAT HAPPENS
19:11-16	
19:17-18	
19:19-21	
20:1-3	
20:4-10	
20:11-15	

COMMENTARY

Prelude to final victory: 19:1-10
Choruses full of praise to God break into the angel's lone song of mourning over Babylon's fall. The heavenly choir has reason to sing: God has judged with justice (19:2) and the people of faith have been reunited with the Lamb (19:6-8).

For corrupting the earth and shedding the blood of the saints, Babylon—looking like Sodom and Gomorrah of long ago—is consigned to an everlasting fire.

For its faithful, suffering witness, the people of the Lamb prepare to celebrate their perfected covenant in a joyous wedding feast with their Lord.

Scene 1: Rider on the white horse: 19:11-16
In heaven, Christ suddenly appears. All details enhance his status as Lord and his role as righteous judge.

Scene 2: Word to the birds: 19:17-18
Christ's appearance inspires another warning of impending doom for his enemies on earth. In grim contrast to the joyous supper of the Lamb (19:9), the vultures of the air prepare to feast on the followers of the beast.

Scene 3: Into the lake of burning sulfur: 19:19-21
Twice before we saw the forces of evil mustering for a last battle against Christ at Armageddon (16:12-14, 16; 17:12-14). Now the time for that battle has arrived.

But be sure to note this: *there is no battle!* Totally powerless at the revelation of the world's true Lord, the beasts are tossed like pebbles to their permanent destruction in the lake of fire. Their human followers fall at a mere word from the Lord's mouth.

Our author many times has told us why a bloody Armageddon at the end of history will not be necessary. Christ has already conquered. The decisive battle with evil was fought and won at the cross. Now just the appearance of

Christ and the mark of his shed blood (19:13) are enough to spell evil's doom.

Scene 4: Satan sealed in the Abyss: 20:1-3

Now Satan himself is paralyzed at Christ's appearance. In his removal from earth, Christ's direct action is not even needed. A lone angel can bind Satan and lock him in the Abyss.

Again we hear Revelation's amazing good news: in spite of his present fury, Satan one day will cower helplessly before the world's only true Lord.

Scene 5: Christ reigns: 20:4-10

The faithful church proceeds to receive its just due. It is raised to life. Those who have bound their lives to the Lamb are lifted up with their Lord. John singles out the martyrs for special recognition (20:4b).

Scenes 4-5 together, and the figure "1,000 years" (20:4d-5), point to a future time in our world's history when the present lordship of Christ will be made visible and real in all spheres of life. Revelation consistently has taught that God's saving purposes are *for* the world—not *from* the world. In the thousand-year banishment of Satan and reign of Christ and his church, we see the fulfillment of Jesus' prayer, "Your kingdom come, your will be done *on earth* as it is in heaven."

The scene closes with a brief release of Satan, his abortive attack on the resurrected church, and his banishment from the earth. Again Satan's true weakness is exposed. A mere bolt from heaven cuts short the attack of his wicked spiritual army (Gog and Magog), while the world's deceiver himself is easily cast into the lake of fire. This final release of Satan may express John's belief that even under the visible lordship of Christ, our world still will contain the potential for evil. But our author's main purpose has been to restate yet again his overarching themes: evil in the end will be destroyed, and God's people will be saved.

Scene 6: Death and the dead are judged: 20:11-15
Again God's righteous law is fulfilled, as "the dead" stand before the throne to receive their just due. Since the church has already risen to life, the emphasis here is on the fate of those not numbered among the Lamb's people. Their sentencing to the lake of fire is not God's final act of punishment. Rather, their fate is merely the climax of their choice to live outside of God's law. Since these loyalists of the beast have remained unrepentant through the long period of God's first judgment, God for one last time "gives them over" to the rewards of their sin.

Death quickly follows them to its own destruction in the lake of fire. With the disappearance of this last great enemy, evil has been purged from the world, and the stage is set for the new creation which God has been building since Christ.

GOING DEEPER

Earlier in our study of Revelation, we met some rather specific predictions, promises, and foreshadowings of future events. To help us see chapters 19—20 from the point of view of the total book, complete the following exercise. Look up and summarize the following references.

REVELATION PREDICTS THE FUTURE	HOW FULFILLED IN CHAPTERS 19—20
1:7	
2:26-27	

3:5

_____ _____

3:21

_____ _____

5:10

_____ _____

11:15

_____ _____

11:18

_____ _____

2. Let's reflect more on the picture of Christ in 19:11-16.

What is he called? _____

What is the color of his horse? _____
Where did we see a horse of the same color earlier?
_____

How does this rider and horse differ from that earlier one?
_____

From what Revelation has taught us about the nature of evil, why does it seem fitting that the earlier horse was the same color as Christ's?
_____
_____

96 / NEW HEAVEN ON A NEW EARTH

What name is on his robe and thigh?

Who knows this name? _____
What do these two names imply for the people and nations of earth?

How does he judge and how does he make war?

Where did the blood on his robe come from?

What kind of sword does he use to strike down the nations?

Describe the battle, if any, that this rider wages against the beast and his armies (19:19-20)?

From these observations, what general conclusion do you draw about how God through Christ has dealt with and *will* in the end deal with evil?

A stanza of Martin Luther's "A Mighty Fortress Is Our God" goes as follows: "And though this world, with devils filled should threaten to undo us/ We will not fear, for God hath willed His truth to triumph through us/ The prince of darkness grim, We tremble not for him/ His rage we can endure;/ For lo, his doom is sure/ One little word shall fell him." Would John have considered this sound doctrine? Why or why not?

SESSION 12 / 97

_____

_____

_____

3. In light of the above exercise, how does the description of Satan differ from the description of Christ?

_____

_____

What meaning does this have for our personal faith and our everyday way of life as believers?

_____

_____

4. Find and note the meaning of the scenes which picture the climax of these central themes of Revelation.

the defeat of evil: _____

_____

_____

the victory of the faithful church: _____

_____

_____

the full realization in history of Christ's lordship:

_____

_____

5. What could the scenes of these chapters have meant to Revelation's first readers?

_____

_____
_____
to us? _____
_____
_____
_____

Session 13. God at home in the glistening city

Revelation 21—22

In his closing vision of a new Jerusalem as the centerpiece of a renewed creation, our author reveals the goal of God's redemptive work. This is the purpose for which the Lamb was slain and the goal to which the Lamb's people by their patient endurance have witnessed.

GETTING STARTED

The new Jerusalem
1. Get acquainted with John's vision of the new Jerusalem by noting the details of the city.

21:2: where it comes from _____

21:2: what it resembles _____

21:3: who will live there _____

21:11: what it shines with _____

21:12-14: what surrounds it _____

21:16: the shape of the city _____

21:18: what it is made of _____

21:19: what decorates its foundations _____

100 / NEW HEAVEN ON A NEW EARTH

21:21: what its gates are made of _____

21:23: the source of its light _____

21:24: who walks in it _____

21:25: the position of its gates _____

21:27: who will enter it _____

22:1: what flows down its great street _____

22:2: what stands on each side _____

22:3: what will be in the city _____

22:3b-4: what God's servants will do there

_____

22:5b: what will give the servants light

_____

22:5c: what else these servants will do

_____

2. Note also what the new Jerusalem *does not* contain.

21:1c _____

21:4 _____

21:8 _____

21:22 _____

21:23 _____

21:25b _____

21:27 _____

22:3a _____

22:5a _____

3. What impression does this vision create for you?

_____

COMMENTARY

A world fully redeemed
Looking forward to the end of history, John sees a fully redeemed world in which the old heaven and earth have been remade and have become one. This new world is notable both for what it lacks and for what it contains. Gone is the sea—that reservoir of evil out of which the beast had emerged (21:1). Also gone are the sufferings experienced by God's people in their strenuous witness for the Lamb against the beast (21:4).

God at home in the glistening city
At the heart of this renewed creation glistens a city: the new Jerusalem. Prophets before John had seen the end of history as a rebuilt Jerusalem on Mount Zion, which would glow with God's presence and be filled with the worship of God. (For example, see Isa. 2:1-4, 54:11-15, 60:1-3; Ezek. 40-43.)

Our author foresees the fulfillment of these prophecies, but in a broader, richer, deeper way. This new Jerusalem is not the literal Jerusalem on Mount Zion restored at some future time. This city comes down from heaven; it does not arise from earth. It is created by God, not humans, and has roots in no earthly locale. This Jerusalem is a *symbol* of the great community of salvation, embracing faithful Jews *and* Gentiles, when God's saving purposes have been fulfilled.

The distinguishing feature of the new Jerusalem is God's direct presence. God lives here with humanity! So intimate and direct is the bond between God and its citizens that they see God's face (22:4).

All physical details of the city enhance this basic feature of perfect, blessed community between God and people. Its walls suggest security for its inhabitants. The precious stones and jewels mirror the city's inner glory. The cubical dimensions (21:16) allude to the cube-shaped holy of holies of the old temple. This inner chamber, where God's presence dwelt, could be entered only by the high priest, and only on the annual Day of Atonement. But now, in the new Jerusalem, the whole city is a holy of holies! Everyone has direct access to God's presence. For this reason, the city has no need for a temple (21:22).

Finally, the city's river, whose source is God's throne, waters trees of life which harken back to an earlier garden called Eden, where God and people once enjoyed perfect communion. John's imagery implies that the new Jerusalem will be a new Eden, in which the present distress in creation will be overcome.

An open city for the overcomers
The way into the new Jerusalem is at the same time wide and narrow. On the one hand, the city is radically open. Its gates are never shut (21:25); all who are thirsty may come in (22:17). John even sees on its streets the nations and kings of the earth (21:24). In Revelation, these groups have consistently opposed the Lamb. Their mention here is yet another clue that somehow, at the climax of God's redemptive work, even the most hardhearted of enemies may yet come to be saved.

On the other hand, entry requirements must be met, and they are strict. Twice we read lists of those denied admission (21:8, 22:15). They who "overcome" (21:7), whose names are inscribed in the Lamb's book (21:27), and who "wash their robes" (22:14) will inhabit the city and share its blessings.

New Jerusalem now
Revelation's overall teaching about the church's hope ought to expand our view of the scope and time of eternal

life. Its closing vision reminds us that God's saving activity through Christ seeks more than the redemption of random, individual souls. God's salvation embraces all of creation, issuing in a purified *world* (21:1). This new heaven and earth will be peopled by a *community* drawn together around God by the Lamb.

What's more, Revelation has taught that this new world and community are not purely future realities. They begin *now*, within God's kingdom of priests (1:6), that new Israel (7:4) which witnesses patiently and faithfully to the Lamb and thereby exhibits the firstfruits of this new creation (14:4c).

In light of this end to which it and the world is destined, the prayer of that faithful church cannot but be, "Come Lord Jesus" (22:20).

GOING DEEPER

1. The new Jerusalem is the second major city we have seen in Revelation. The first was Babylon the Great. Our author seems to contrast them deliberately. Note some of the differences.

BABYLON	NEW JERUSALEM
prostitute (17:1)	21:2: _____
rooted in beast (17:3b)	21:2: _____
dressed in purple, scarlet (17:4a)	21:2: _____
cup of abominations (17:4b)	22:1: _____
object of kings' adultery (17:2)	21:24: _____

intoxicates inhabitants of
   earth (17:2)   22:2: _____

murdered the saints (17:6) 21:24: _____

devoured by beast (17:16) 21:2: _____

home for demons, evil
spirits, unclean birds
   (18:1)   21:27: _____

2. Observe the gates and foundations of the new Jerusalem (21:12-14).

Whose name was found on the gates? _____

_____

on the foundations? _____

What number is repeated several times? _____

We have suggested that the new Jerusalem is a symbol for the broad community of God's faithful people at the end of time. How do the details you have just observed support that view?

_____

_____

_____

_____

3. Let's think more about those who enter the city and those who are excluded from it. Can you recall from our study specific illustrations of the types of people mentioned in 21:8 who are barred from entry? If so, write them on the appropriate line:

cowardly _____

unbelieving _____

vile _____

murderers _____

sexually immoral _____

practitioners of magic arts _____

idolaters _____

liars _____
Recall the qualifications for entry into the city (21:7, 27; 22:14). How has Revelation sharpened our understanding of what these mean for us?

_____
_____
_____
_____

4. Consider the warning of 22:18-19. What do you think it means to "add to" or "take away from" the Book of Revelation?

_____
_____
_____
_____

5. According to what Revelation has taught us, what difference should the promise of 22:20 make in our Christian lives?

_____
_____
_____
_____

Books

Commentaries on Revelation

Barclay, William. *The Revelation of John.* (The Daily Study Bible, 2 volumes.) Toronto: G. R. Welch & Co., Ltd., 1976.

Beasley-Murray, G. R. *The Book of Revelation.* (New Century Bible.) London: Oliphants, 1974.

Caird, G. B. *The Revelation of St. John the Divine.* (Harper's New Testament Commentaries.) New York: Harper & Row, 1966.

Eller, Vernard. *The Most Revealing Book of the Bible.* Grand Rapids: William B. Eerdmans, 1974.

Ladd, George Eldon. *A Commentary on the Revelation of John.* Grand Rapids: William B. Eerdmans, 1972.

Mounce, Robert H. *The Book of Revelation.* (The New International Commentary on the New Testament.) Grand Rapids: William B. Eerdmans, 1977.

Schussler Fiorenza, Elisabeth. *Invitation to the Book of Revelation.* Garden City: Image Books, 1981.

Books on Related Themes

Erb, Paul. *Bible Prophecy.* Scottdale: Herald Press, 1978.

Ewert, David. *And Then Comes the End.* Scottdale: Herald Press, 1980.